Erich Fromm ... psychoanalyst and author of suc... ...ual books as **The Art of Loving, Escape from Freedom, The Heart of Man, Beyond the Chains of Illusion,** and **Man for Himself.** Born in Frankfurt, Germany, in 1900, he studied at the Universities of Heidelberg and Munich, and at the Psychoanalytic Institute in Berlin. He has taught in Germany and Mexico, and in the United States at Bennington College, Yale University, Michigan State University and New York University.

THE REVOLUTION OF HOPE, Dr. Fromm says, "is addressed to the reader very directly and to what he really feels and thinks, very much in the style of **The Art of Loving.**" In this book, Dr. Fromm discusses the specific problems of the individual today: the problems of youth, born into a society which is urgently in need of change; the problems of "modern industrial man . . . trapped in meaningless work and compulsive consumption"; the problems of *human* life in a mechanized and technologized society whose politics and morals have become corrupt. In its boldness, originality and affirmation of hope, this book speaks both to the insurgent young and to the elders who share their concerns.

This Bantam Books edition
reprints volume XXXVIII of the
WORLD PERSPECTIVES SERIES
which is planned and edited
by Ruth Nanda Anshen. Dr. Anshen's
epilogue to this reprint appears
on page 171.

ERICH FROMM
THE REVOLUTION OF HOPE

TOWARD A HUMANIZED TECHNOLOGY

BANTAM BOOKS · TORONTO · NEW YORK · LONDON

This low-priced Bantam Book
has been completely reset in a type face
designed for easy reading, and was
printed from new plates. It contains the complete
text of the original hard-cover edition.
NOT ONE WORD HAS BEEN OMITTED.

THE REVOLUTION OF HOPE
A Bantam Book / published by arrangement with
Harper & Row, Publishers, Inc.

PRINTING HISTORY
Harper & Row edition published October 1968
Bantam edition published October 1968
2nd printing
3rd printing

Bantam Books are published by Bantam Books, Inc., a subsidiary
of Grosset & Dunlap, Inc. Its trade-mark, consisting of the words
"Bantam Books" and the portrayal of a bantam, is registered in the
United States Patent Office and in other countries. Marca Registrada.
Bantam Books, Inc., 271 Madison Avenue, New York, N.Y. 10016.

PRINTED IN THE UNITED STATES OF AMERICA

Contents

Foreword

This book is written as a response to America's situation in the year 1968. It is born out of the conviction that we are at the crossroads: one road leads to a completely mechanized society with man as a helpless cog in the machine—if not to destruction by thermonuclear war; the other to a renaissance of humanism and hope—to a society that puts technique in the service of man's well-being.

This book is meant to clarify the issues for those who have not clearly recognized our dilemma, and it is an appeal to action. It is based on the conviction that we can find the necessary new solutions with the help of reason and passionate love for life, and not through irrationality and hate. It is addressed to a broad spectrum of readers with different political and religious concepts but sharing this concern for life and respect for reason and reality.

This book, like all my previous work, attempts to distinguish between individual and social reality and the ideologies that misuse and "coopt" valuable ideas for the purpose of supporting the *status quo*. For many of the young generation who belittle the value of traditional thought, I should like to stress my conviction that even the most radical development must have its continuity with the past; that we cannot progress by throwing away the best achievements of the human mind—and that to be young is not enough!

Since this book deals with topics I have dealt with in various works in the past forty years, I could not avoid mentioning many of the same ideas. They are reorganized around the central issue: the alternatives to dehumanization. But this book contains also many new ideas that go beyond my previous thinking.

Since I am writing for a large audience, I have reduced quotations to the bare minimum, but I have quoted all authors who have influenced my thinking in writing this book. As a rule, I have also not made reference to those of my books which have a direct relevance to the material dealt with here. These are especially: *Escape from Freedom* (Holt, Rinehart and Winston, 1941), *Man for Himself* (Holt, Rinehart and Winston, 1947), *The Sane Society* (Holt, Rinehart and Winston, 1955), *The Heart of Man* (Harper & Row, 1964).

The general approach taken in this book reflects the character of the central problem under consideration. While this is as it should be, it may at times pose some minor difficulty for the reader. The work attempts to bring together two problem areas that are often treated separately—human character structure, qualities, and potentialities, and contemporary social, political, and economic problems. The emphasis differs from section to section, but throughout a major objective is to integrate and interweave these discussions. This is done in the firm belief that a realistic and successful approach to the problems of contemporary American society is only possible if the analysis of our whole social system includes what is called in this book "the system Man." I hope the reader will respond by overcoming the thought habits of compartmentalization and not find it too difficult to accompany me in the jumps from "psychology" to "sociology" and "politics," and back again.

It remains to express my thanks to those who have read the whole manuscript repeatedly and made many editorial suggestions—to Ruth Nanda Anshen, to my wife, and to Raymond G. Brown, who in addition has assisted me with valuable suggestions in the field of economics. I also want to express my thanks to the publishers for their special efforts, which made it possible for the book to be published ten weeks after delivery of the manuscript.

E.F.

THE REVOLUTION OF HOPE

Toward a Humanized Technology

Chapter I

The Crossroads

A specter is stalking in our midst whom only a few see with clarity. It is not the old ghost of communism or fascism. It is a new specter: a completely mechanized society, devoted to maximal material output and consumption, directed by computers; and in this social process, man himself is being transformed into a part of the total machine, well fed and entertained, yet passive, unalive, and with little feeling. With the victory of the new society, individualism and privacy will have disappeared; feelings toward others will be engineered by psychological conditioning and other devices, or drugs which also serve a new kind of introspective experience. As Zbigniew Brzezinski put it, "In the technetronic society the trend would seem to be towards the aggregation of the individual support of millions of uncoordinated citizens, easily within the reach of magnetic and attractive personalities effectively exploiting the latest communication techniques to manipulate emotions and control reason." [1] This new form of society has been predicted in the form of fiction in Orwell's *1984* and Aldous Huxley's *Brave New World*.

Perhaps its most ominous aspect at present is that we seem to lose control over our own system. We execute the decisions which our computer calculations make for us. We as human beings have no aims except producing and consuming more and more. We will nothing, nor do we not-will anything. We are threatened with extinc-

---

[1] "The Technetronic Society," *Encounter*, Vol. XXX, No. 1 (January, 1968), p. 19.

tion by nuclear weapons and with inner deadness by the passiveness which our exclusion from responsible decision making engenders.

How did it happen? How did man, at the very height of his victory over nature, become the prisoner of his own creation and in serious danger of destroying himself?

In the search for scientific truth, man came across knowledge that he could use for the domination of nature. He had tremendous success. But in the one-sided emphasis on technique and material consumption, man lost touch with himself, with life. Having lost religious faith and the humanistic values bound up with it, he concentrated on technical and material values and lost the capacity for deep emotional experiences, for the joy and sadness that accompany them. The machine he built became so powerful that it developed its own program, which now determines man's own thinking.

At the moment, one of the gravest symptoms of our system is the fact that our economy rests upon arms production (plus maintenance of the whole defense establishment) and on the principle of maximal consumption. We have a well-functioning economic system under the condition that we are producing goods which threaten us with physical destruction, that we transform the individual into a total passive consumer and thus deaden him, and that we have created a bureaucracy which makes the individual feel impotent.

Are we confronted with a tragic, insolvable dilemma? *Must we produce sick people in order to have a healthy economy, or can we use our material resources, our inventions, our computers to serve the ends of man? Must individuals be passive and dependent in order to have strong and well-functioning organizations?*

The answers to these questions differ. Among those who recognize the revolutionary and drastic change in human life which the "megamachine" could bring about are the writers who say that the new society is unavoidable, and hence that there is no point in arguing about its merits. At the same time, they are sympathetic to the new society, although they express slight misgivings about what it might do to man as we know him. Zbigniew Brzezinski and H. Kahn are representatives of this attitude. On the other end of the spectrum is Jacques Ellul, who in his *Technological Society* describes with great force the new society which we are approaching and its destructive influence on man. He faces the specter in its dreadful lack of humanness. His conclusion is not that the new society is bound to win, although he thinks that, in terms of probabilities, it is likely to win. But he sees a possibility that the dehumanized society may not be the victor "if an increasing number of people become fully aware of the threat the technological world poses to man's personal and spiritual life, and if they determine to assert their freedom by upsetting the course of this evolution." [2] Lewis Mumford's position may be considered similar to that of Ellul. In his profound and brilliant *The Myth of the Machine*,[3] he describes the "megamachine," starting with its first manifestations in Egyptian and Babylonian societies. But in contrast to those who, like the previously mentioned authors, recognize the specter with either sympathy or horror are the majority of men, those at the top of the establishment and the average citizen, who do not see a specter. They have the old-fashioned belief of the nineteenth century that the machine will help lighten man's burden, that it will remain a means to an end, and they do not see the danger that if technology is permitted to follow its own logic, it will become a cancerlike growth, eventually threatening the structured system of individual and social life. The position taken in this book [4] is in principle that of Mumford and Ellul. It is perhaps different in the

---

[2] French edition, 1954; American edition, 1964, Alfred Knopf, and first Vintage Books edition, 1967, p. xxx.

[3] Lewis Mumford, *The Myth of the Machine* (New York: Harcourt, Brace & World, 1966).

[4] As in *Escape from Freedom* and *The Sane Society*.

sense that I see a somewhat greater possibility of restoring the social system to man's control. My hopes in this respect are based on the following factors:

1. The present social system can be understood a great deal better if one connects the system "Man" with the whole system. Human nature is not an abstraction nor an infinitely malleable and hence dynamically negligible system. It has its own specific qualities, laws, and alternatives. The study of the system Man permits us to see what certain factors in the socioeconomic system do to man, how disturbances in the system Man produce imbalances in the whole social system. By introducing the human factor into the analysis of the whole system, we are better prepared to understand its dysfunctioning and to define norms which relate the healthy economic functioning of the social system to the optimal well-being of the people who participate in it. All this is valid, of course, only if there is agreement that maximal development of the human system in terms of its own structure —that is to say, human well-being—is the overriding goal.

2. The increasing dissatisfaction with our present way of life, its passiveness and silent boredom, its lack of privacy and its depersonalization, and the longing for a joyful, meaningful existence, which answers those specific needs of man which he has developed in the last few thousand years of his history and which make him different from the animal as well as from the computer. This tendency is all the stronger because the affluent part of the population has already tasted full material satisfaction and has found out that the consumer's paradise does not deliver the happiness it promised. (The poor, of course, have not yet had any chance to find out, except by watching the lack of joy of those who "have everything a man could want.")

Ideologies and concepts have lost much of their attraction; traditional clichés like "right" and "left" or "communism" and "capitalism" have lost their meaning. People seek a new orientation, a new philosophy, one which is centered on the priorities of life—physically and spiritually—and not on the priorities of death.

There is a growing polarization occurring in the United States and in the whole world: There are those who are attracted to force, "law and order," bureaucratic methods, and eventually to non-life, and those with a deep longing for life, for new attitudes rather than for ready-made schemes and blueprints. This new front is a movement which combines the wish for profound changes in our economic and social practice with changes in our psychic and spiritual approach to life. In its most general form, its aim is the activation of the individual, the restoration of man's control over the social system, the humanization of technology. It is a movement in the name of life, and it has such a broad and common base because the threat to life is today a threat not to one class, to one nation, but a threat to all.

The following chapters attempt to discuss in detail some of the problems outlined here, specifically those which have to do with the relation between human nature and the socioeconomic system.

There is, however, one point that must be clarified first. Today a widespread hopelessness exists with regard to the possibility of changing the course we have taken. This hopelessness is mainly unconscious, while consciously people are "optimistic" and hope for further "progress." The discussion of the present situation and its potential for hope should be preceded by a discussion of the phenomenon of hope.

Chapter II

Hope

1. WHAT HOPE IS NOT

Hope is a decisive element in any attempt to bring about social change in the direction of greater aliveness, awareness, and reason. But the nature of hope is often misunderstood and confused with attitudes that have nothing to do with hope and in fact are the very opposite.

What is it to hope?

Is it, as many think, to have desires and wishes? If this were so, those who desire more and better cars, houses, and gadgets would be people of hope. But they are not; they are people lusty for more consumption and not people of hope.

Is it to hope if hope's object is not a thing but a fuller life, a state of greater aliveness, a liberation from eternal boredom; or, to use a theological term, for salvation; or, a political term, for revolution? Indeed, this kind of expectation could be hope; but it is non-hope if it has the quality of passiveness, and "waiting for"—until the hope becomes, in fact, a cover for resignation, a mere ideology.

Kafka has beautifully described this kind of resigned and passive hope in a story in *The Trial*. A man comes to the door leading into heaven (the Law) and begs admittance from the doorkeeper. The doorkeeper says he cannot admit the man at the moment. Although the door leading into the Law stands open, the man decides that he had better wait until he gets permission to enter. So he sits down and waits for days and years. He repeatedly asks to be allowed in, but is always told that he cannot be allowed to enter yet. During all these long years the man studies the doorkeeper almost incessantly and learns to know even the fleas in his fur collar. Eventually, he is old and near death. For the first time, he asks the question, "How does it come about that in all these years no one has come seeking admittance but me?" The doorkeeper answers, "No one but you could gain admittance through this door, since this door was intended for you. I am now going to shut it."

The old man was too old to understand, and maybe he would not have understood if he had been younger. The bureaucrats have the last word; if they say no, he cannot enter. If he had had more than this passive, waiting hope, he would have entered and his courage to disregard the bureaucrats would have been the liberating act which would have carried him to the shining palace. Many people are like Kafka's old man. They hope, but it is not given to them to act upon their heart's impulse, and as long as the bureaucrats do not give the green light, they wait and wait.[1]

This kind of passive hope is closely related to a generalized form of hope, which might be described as hoping for *time*. Time and the future become the central category of this kind of hope. Nothing is expected to happen in the *now* but only in the next moment, the next day, the next year, and in another world if it is too absurd to believe that hope can be realized in this world. Behind this belief is the idolatry of "Future," "History," and "Posterity," which began in the French Revolution with men like Robespierre, who worshiped the future as a goddess: I do nothing; I remain passive, because I am nothing and impotent; but the future, the projection of time, will bring about what I cannot achieve. This worship of the future, which is a different aspect of the

---

[1] The Spanish word *esperar* means at the same time waiting and hoping, and quite clearly it refers to that particular kind of passive hope that I am trying to describe here.

worship of "progress" in modern bourgeois thought, is precisely the alienation of hope. Instead of something I do or I become, the idols, future and posterity, bring about something without my doing anything.[2]

While passive waiting is a disguised form of hopelessness and impotence, there is another form of hopelessness and despair which takes exactly the opposite disguise—the disguise of phrase making and adventurism, of disregard for reality, and of forcing what cannot be forced. This was the attitude of the false Messiahs and of the *Putsch* leaders, who had contempt for those who did not under all circumstances prefer death to defeat. In these days, the pseudo-radical disguise of hopelessness and nihilism is not rare among some of the most dedicated members of the young generation. They are appealing in their boldness and dedication but they become unconvincing by their lack of realism, sense of strategy, and, in some, by lack of love for life.[3]

---

[2] The Stalinist concept that history decides what is right and wrong and good and evil is a direct continuation of Robespierre's idolatry of posterity. It is the extreme opposite of the position of Marx, who said, "History is nothing and does nothing. It is man who is and does." Or, in the Theses on Feuerbach, "The materialist doctrine that men are products of circumstances and upbringing, and that, therefore, changed men are products of other circumstances and changed upbringing, forgets that it is men that change circumstances and that the educator himself needs educating."

[3] Such hopelessness shines through Herbert Marcuse's *Eros and Civilization* (Boston: Beacon Press, 1955) and *One-Dimensional Man* (Beacon Press, 1964). All traditional values, like love, tenderness, concern, and responsibility, are supposed to have had meaning only in a pretechnological society. In the new technological society—one without repression and exploitation—a new man will arrive who will not have to be afraid of anything, including death, who will develop yet-unspecified needs, and who will have a chance to satisfy his "polymorphous sexuality" (I refer the reader to Freud's *Three Contributions to the Theory of Sex*); briefly, the final progress of man is seen in the regression to infantile life, the return to the happiness of the satiated baby. No wonder that Marcuse ends up in hopelessness. "The critical theory of society possesses no concepts which

2. THE PARADOX AND NATURE OF HOPE

Hope is *paradoxical*. It is neither passive waiting nor is it unrealistic forcing of circumstances that cannot occur. It is like the crouched tiger, which will jump only when the moment for jumping has come. Neither tired reformism nor pseudo-radical adventurism is an expression of hope. To hope means to be ready at every moment for that which is not yet born, and yet not become desperate if there is no birth in our lifetime. There is no sense in hoping for that which already exists or for that which cannot be. Those whose hope is weak settle down for comfort or for violence; those whose hope is strong see and cherish all signs of new life and are ready every moment to help the birth of that which is ready to be born.

Among the confusions about hope one of the major ones is the failure to distinguish between conscious and unconscious hope. This is an error, of course, which

---

could bridge the gap between the present and its future; holding no promise and showing no success, it remains negative. Thus it wants to remain loyal to those who, without hope, have given and give their life to the Great Refusal" (*One-Dimensional Man*, p. 257).

These quotations show how wrong those are who attack or admire Marcuse as a revolutionary leader; for revolution was never based on hopelessness, nor can it ever be. But Marcuse is not even concerned with politics; for if one is not concerned with steps between the present and the future, one does not deal with politics, radical or otherwise. Marcuse is essentially an example of an alienated intellectual, who presents his personal despair as a theory of radicalism. Unfortunately, his lack of understanding and, to some extent, knowledge of Freud builds a bridge over which he travels to synthesize Freudianism, bourgeois materialism, and sophisticated Hegelianism into what to him and other like-minded "radicals" seems to be the most progressive theoretical construct. This is not the place to show in detail that it is a naïve, cerebral daydream, essentially irrational, unrealistic, and lacking love of life.

occurs with regard to many other emotional experiences, such as happiness, anxiety, depression, boredom, and hate. It is amazing that in spite of the popularity of Freud's theories his concept of the unconscious has been so little applied to such emotional phenomena. There are perhaps two main reasons for this fact. One is that in the writings of some psychoanalysts and some "philosophers of psychoanalysis" the whole phenomenon of the unconscious—that is, of repression—refers to sexual desires, and they use repression—wrongly—as synonymous with *suppression* of sexual wishes and activities. In doing so they deprive Freud's discoveries of some of their most important consequences. The second reason lies probably in the fact that it is far less disturbing for the post-Victorian generations to become aware of repressed sexual desires than of those experiences like alienation, hopelessness, or greed. To use only one of the most obvious examples: most people do not admit to themselves feelings of fear, boredom, loneliness, hopelessness—that is to say, they are *unconscious* [4] of these feelings. This is so for a simple reason. Our social pattern is such that the successful man is not supposed to be afraid or bored or lonely. He must find this world the best of all worlds; in order to have the best chance for promotion he must repress fear as well as doubt, depression, boredom, or hopelessness.

There are many who feel consciously hopeful and unconsciously hopeless, and there are a few for whom it is the other way around. What matters in the examination of hope and hopelessness is not primarily what people *think* about their feelings, but what they truly feel. This can be recognized least from their words and phrases, but can be detected from their facial expressions, their

---

[4] I want to stress that speaking of "the unconscious" is another form of alienated thinking and speaking. There is no such thing as "the unconscious," as if it were an organ or a thing in space. One can be "conscious of" or "unconscious of" outer or inner events; that is, we deal with a psychic *function,* not with a localized *organ.*

way of walking, their capacity to react with interest to something in front of their eyes, and their lack of fanaticism, which is shown in their ability to listen to reasonable argument.

The dynamic viewpoint applied in this book to social-psychological phenomena is fundamentally different from the descriptive behaviorist approach in most social-science research. From the dynamic standpoint, we are not primarily interested in knowing what a person thinks or says or how he behaves *now*. We are interested in his character structure—that is, in the semipermanent structure of his energies, in the directions in which they are channeled, and in the intensity with which they flow. If we know the driving forces motivating behavior, not only do we understand present behavior but we can also make reasonable assumptions about how a person is likely to act under changed circumstances. In the dynamic view, surprising "changes" in a person's thought or behavior are changes which mostly could have been foreseen, given the knowledge of his character structure.

More could be said about what hope is *not,* but let us press forward and ask what hope is. Can it be described at all in words or can it only be communicated in a poem, in a song, in a gesture, in a facial expression, or in a deed?

As with every other human experience, words are insufficient to describe the experience. In fact, most of the time words do the opposite: they obscure it, dissect it, and kill it. Too often, in the process of talking about love or hate or hope, one loses contact with what one was supposed to be talking about. Poetry, music, and other forms of art are by far the best-suited media for describing human experience because they are precise and avoid the abstraction and vagueness of worn-out coins which are taken for adequate representations of human experience.

Yet, taking these qualifications seriously, it is not impossible to touch upon feeling experience in words

which are not those of poetry. This would not be possible
if people did not share the experience one talks about,
at least to some degree. To describe it means to point
out the various aspects of the experience and thus to
establish a communication in which the writer and the
reader know that they are referring to the same thing. In
making this attempt, I must ask the reader to work with
me and not expect me to give him an answer to the
question of what hope is. I must ask him to mobilize his
own experiences in order to make our dialogue possible.

To hope is a state of being. It is an inner readiness,
that of intense but not-yet-spent activeness.[5] The concept of "activity" rests upon one of the most widespread
of man's illusions in modern industrial society. Our
whole culture is geared to activity—activity in the
sense of being busy, and being busy in the sense of
busyness (the busyness necessary for business). In fact,
most people are so "active" that they cannot stand doing
nothing; they even transform their so-called leisure time
into another form of activity. If you are not active making money, you are active driving around, playing golf,
or just chatting about nothing. What is dreaded is the
moment in which you have really nothing "to do."
Whether one calls this kind of behavior activity is a
terminological question. The trouble is that most people
who think they are very active are not aware of the fact
that they are intensely passive in spite of their "busyness." They constantly need the stimulus from the outside, be it other people's chatter, or the sight of movies,

---

[5] I owe the term "activeness" (instead of the usual term "activity") to a personal communication from Michael Maccoby;
correspondingly I use the term passiveness instead of passivity,
when activeness or passiveness refers to an attitude or state of
mind.

I have discussed the problem of activity and passivity, especially in connection with the productive orientation, in several
books. I want to call the reader's attention to the excellent and
profound discussion of activity and passivity in *Metamorphosis*
by Ernest Schachtel (New York: Basic Books, 1959).

or travel and other forms of more thrilling consumption excitements, even if it is only a new man or woman as a sexual partner. They need to be prompted, to be "turned on," tempted, seduced. They always run and never stand. They always "fall for" and never get up. And they imagine themselves to be immensely active while they are driven by the obsession to do something in order to escape the anxiety that is aroused when they are confronted with themselves.

Hope is a psychic concomitant to life and growth. If a tree which does not get sun bends its trunk to where the sun comes from, we cannot say that the tree "hopes" in the same way in which a man hopes, since hope in man is connected with feelings and awareness that the tree may not have. And yet it would not be wrong to say that the tree hopes for the sunlight and expresses this hope by twisting its trunk toward the sun. Is it different with the child that is born? He may have no awareness, yet his activity expresses his hope to be born and to breathe independently. Does the suckling not hope for his mother's breasts? Does the infant not hope to stand erect and to walk? Does the sick man not hope to be well, the prisoner to be free, the hungry to eat? Do we not hope to wake up to another day when we fall asleep? Does love making not imply a man's hope in his potency, in his capacity to arouse his partner, and the woman's hope to respond and to arouse him?

3. FAITH

When hope has gone life has ended, actually or potentially. Hope is an intrinsic element of the structure of life, of the dynamic of man's spirit. It is closely linked with another element of the structure of life: *faith*. Faith is not a weak form of belief or knowledge; it is not faith in this or that; faith is the conviction about the not yet proven, the knowledge of the real possibility, the awareness of pregnancy. Faith is rational when it refers to the knowledge of the real yet unborn; it is based on the faculty of knowledge and comprehension, which penetrates the surface and sees the kernel. Faith, like hope, is not prediction of the *future;* it is the vision of the *present* in a state of pregnancy.

The statement that faith is certainty needs a qualification. It is certainty about the reality of the possibility—but it is not certainty in the sense of unquestionable predictability. The child may be stillborn prematurely; it may die in the act of birth; it may die in the first two weeks of life. This is the paradox of faith: *it is the certainty of the uncertain.*[6] It is certainty in terms of man's vision and comprehension; it is not certainty in terms of the final outcome of reality. We need no faith in that which is scientifically predictable, nor can there be faith in that which is impossible. Faith is based on our experience of living, of transforming ourselves. Faith that others can change is the outcome of the experience that I can change.[7]

There is an important distinction between rational and irrational faith.[8] While rational faith is the result of one's own inner activeness in thought or feeling, irrational faith is submission to something given, which one accepts as true regardless of whether it is or not. The essential element of all irrational faith is its passive character, be its object an idol, a leader, or an ideology. Even the scientist needs to be free from irrational faith in traditional ideas in order to have rational faith in the power of his creative thought. Once his discovery is "proved," he needs no more faith, except in the next step he is contemplating. In the sphere of human relations, "having faith" in another person means to be

---

[6] In Hebrew the word "faith" (*emunah*) means certainty. *Amen* means certainly.

[7] The need for certainty will be discussed in Chapter III.

[8] The meaning of "rational" and "irrational" will be discussed in Chapter IV.

certain of his *core*—that is, of the reliability and unchangeability of his fundamental attitudes. In the same sense we can have faith in ourselves—not in the constancy of our opinions, but in our basic orientation to life, the matrix of our character structure. Such faith is conditioned by the experience of self, by our capacity to say "I" legitimately, by the sense of our identity.

Hope is the mood that accompanies faith. Faith could not be sustained without the mood of hope. Hope can have no base except in faith.

4. FORTITUDE

There is still another element linked with hope and faith in the structure of life: courage, or, as Spinoza called it, fortitude. Fortitude is perhaps the less ambiguous expression, because today courage is more often used to demonstrate the courage to die rather than the courage to live. Fortitude is the capacity to resist the temptation to compromise hope and faith by transforming them—and thus destroying them—into empty optimism or into irrational faith. Fortitude is the capacity to say "no" when the world wants to hear "yes."

But fortitude is not fully understood unless we mention another aspect of it: fearlessness. The fearless person is not afraid of threats, not even of death. But, as so often, the word "fearless" covers several entirely different attitudes. I mention only the three most important ones: First, a person can be fearless because he does not care to live; life is not worth much to him, hence he is fearless when it comes to the danger of dying; but while he is not afraid of death, he may be afraid of life. His fearlessness is based on lack of love of life; he is usually not fearless at all when he is not in the situation of risking his life. In fact, he frequently looks for dangerous situations, in order to avoid his fear of life, of himself, and of people.

A second kind of fearlessness is that of the person who lives in symbiotic submission to an idol, be it a person, an institution, or an idea; the commands of the idol are sacred; they are far more compelling than even the survival commands of his body. If he could disobey or doubt these commands of the idol, he would face 'the danger of losing his identity with the idol; this means he would be running the risk of finding himself utterly isolated, and thus at the verge of insanity. He is willing to die because he is afraid of exposing himself to this danger.

The third kind of fearlessness is to be found in the fully developed person, who rests within himself and loves life. The person who has overcome greed does not cling to any idol or any thing and hence has nothing to lose: he is rich because he is empty, he is strong because he is not the slave of his desires. He can let go of idols, irrational desires, and fantasies, because he is in full touch with reality, inside and outside himself. If such a person has reached full "enlightenment," he is completely fearless. If he has moved toward this goal without having arrived, his fearlessness will also not be complete. But anyone who tries to move toward the state of being fully himself knows that whenever a new step toward fearlessness is made, a sense of strength and joy is awakened that is unmistakable. He feels as if a new phase of life had begun. He can feel the truth of Goethe's lines: "I have put my house on nothing, that's why the whole world is mine." (*Ich hab mein Haus auf nichts gestellt, deshalb gehoert mir die ganze Welt.*)

Hope and faith, being essential qualities of *life,* are by their very nature moving in the direction of transcending the *status quo,* individually and socially. It is one of the qualities of all life that it is in a constant process of change and never remains the same at any given moment.[9] Life that stagnates tends to die; if the stagnation

---

[9] This is not the place to discuss the question of definitions of organic life and inorganic matter, respectively, nor of the bor-

is complete, death has occurred. It follows that life in its moving quality tends to break out of and to overcome the *status quo*. We grow either stronger or weaker, wiser or more foolish, more courageous or more cowardly. Every second is a moment of decision, for the better or the worse. We feed our sloth, greed, or hate, or we starve it. The more we feed it, the stronger it grows; the more we starve it, the weaker it becomes.

What holds true for the individual holds true for a society. It is never static; if it does not grow, it decays; if it does not transcend the *status quo* for the better, it changes for the worse. Often we, the individual or the people who make up a society, have the illusion we could stand still and not alter the given situation in the one or the other direction. This is one of the most dangerous illusions. The moment we stand still, we begin to decay.

5. RESURRECTION

This concept of personal or social transformation allows and even compels us to redefine the meaning of resurrection, without any reference to its theological implications in Christianity. Resurrection in its new meaning—for which the Christian meaning would be one of the possible symbolic expressions—is not the creation of *another reality* after the reality of *this* life, but the transformation of *this* reality in the direction of greater aliveness. Man and society are resurrected every moment in the act of hope and of faith in the here and now; every act of love, of awareness, of compassion is resurrection; every act of sloth, of greed, of selfishness

---

derline between the two. Certainly, from the standpoint of present-day biology and genetics, traditional distinctions have become questionable; but it would be erroneous to assume that these distinctions have lost their validity; they need refinement rather than replacement.

is death. Every moment existence confronts us with the alternatives of resurrection or death; every moment we give an answer. This answer lies not in what we say or think, but in what we are, how we act, where we are moving.

6. MESSIANIC HOPE

Faith and hope and this-worldly resurrection have found their classic expression in the messianic vision of the prophets. They do not predict the *future,* like a Cassandra or the chorus of the Greek tragedy; they see the *present reality* free from the blindfolds of public opinion and authority. They do not want to be prophets but feel compelled to express the voice of their conscience—of their "knowing-with"—to say what possibilities they see and to show the people the alternatives and to warn them. This is all they aspire to do. It is up to the people to take their warning seriously and to change their ways, or to remain deaf and blind—and to suffer. Prophetic language is always the language of alternatives, of choice, and of freedom; it is never that of determinism, for better or worse. The shortest formulation of prophetic alternativism is the verse in Deuteronomy: "I put before you today life and death, and you chose life!" [10]

In the prophetic literature the messianic vision rested upon the tension between "what existed or was still there and that which was becoming and was yet to be." [11] In the postprophetic period a change took place

---

[10] I have dealt with the nature of prophetic alternativism in great detail in *You Shall Be as Gods* (New York: Holt, Rinehart and Winston, 1967). Cf. also in the same book the discussion of the apocalyptic tendency in Jewish messianic thought, in contrast to the original alternativistic one (pp. 121 ff.).

[11] Leo Baeck, *Judaism and Christianity* (New York: The Jewish Publication Society of America, 1958), translated with an introduction by W. Kaufman.

in the meaning of the messianic idea, making its first appearance in the Book of Daniel around 164 B.C. and in pseudo-epigraphical literature which was not incorporated in the collection of the Old Testament. This literature has a "vertical" idea of salvation as against the "horizontal" [12] historical idea of the prophets. The emphasis is on the transformation of the individual and largely on a catastrophic end of history, occurring in a final cataclysm. This apocalyptic version is not that of alternatives but of prediction; not that of freedom but of determinism.

In the later Talmudic or Rabbinical tradition the original prophetic alternativistic vision prevailed. Early Christian thought was more strongly influenced by the apocalyptic version of messianic thought, although, paradoxically, as an institution the Church usually retreated to a position of passive waiting.

Nevertheless in the concept of the "Second Coming" the prophetic concept remained alive and the prophetic interpretation of Christian faith has again and again found its expression in revolutionary and "heretical" sects; today the radical wing in the Roman Catholic Church, as well as in the various non-Catholic Christian denominations, shows a marked return to the prophetic principle, to its alternativism as well as to the concept that spiritual aims must be applied to the political and social process. Outside of the Church, original Marxist socialism was the most significant expression of the messianic vision in a secular language, only to be corrupted and destroyed by the communist distortion of Marx. In recent years the messianic element in Marxism has found its voice again in a number of socialist humanists, especially in Yugoslavia, Poland, Czechoslovakia, and Hungary. Marxists and Christians have become en-

---

[12] These terms have been used by Baeck, *op. cit.* Teilhard de Chardin in *The Future of Man* (New York: Harper & Row, 1964) has attempted to construct a synthesis of these concepts.

gaged in a world-wide dialogue, based on the common messianic heritage.[13]

7. THE SHATTERING OF HOPE

If hope, faith, and fortitude are concomitants of life, how is it that so many lose hope, faith, and fortitude and love their servitude and dependence? It is precisely the possibility of this loss that is characteristic of the human existence. We start out with hope, faith, and fortitude—they are the unconscious, "no-thought" qualities of the sperm and the egg, of their union, of the growth of the foetus, its birth. But when life begins, the vicissitudes of environment and accident begin to further or to block the potential of hope.

Most of us had hoped to be loved—not just to be coddled and to be fed, but to be understood, to be cared for, to be respected. Most of us hoped to be able to trust. When we were little we did not yet know the human invention of the lie—not only that of lying with words but that of lying with one's voice, one's gesture, one's eyes, one's facial expression. How should the child be

---

[13] Ernst Bloch, in *Das Prinzip Hoffnung* (*The Principle of Hope*), has more than anyone else recaptured the prophetic principle of hope in Marxist thought. A large number of the contemporary humanist-socialist authors have contributed to the volume *Symposium on Socialist Humanism,* edited by Erich Fromm (New York: Doubleday, 1965). Cf. also the English edition of the Yugoslav journal *Praxis,* and *Dialogue,* edited by G. Nenning, an international review published by *Forum,* which contains a dialogue between Christian and non-Christian Humanists. The widespread assumption that Marx had a deterministic view of history, which said that socialism was inevitable, in my opinion is not correct. The impression of determinism arises from some formulations of Marx, which have their roots in his propagandistic, exhorting style, which is often intermingled with his analytic, scientific one. Rosa Luxemburg, perhaps the most brilliant of Marx's theoretical interpreters, stressed the alternativistic viewpoint in the formulation of the "alternative between Socialism and Barbarism."

For to him that is joined to all the living there is hope.

Ecclesiastes 9:4

prepared for this specifically human ingenuity: the lie? Most of us are awakened, some more and some less brutally, to the fact that people often do not mean what they say or say the opposite of what they mean. And not only "people," but the very people we trusted most —our parents, teachers, leaders.

Few people escape the fate that at one point or another in their development their hopes are disappointed —sometimes completely shattered. Perhaps this is good. If a man did not experience the disappointment of his hope, how could his hope become strong and unquenchable? How could he avoid the danger of being an optimistic dreamer? But on the other hand, hope often is shattered so thoroughly that a man may never recover it.

In fact, the responses and reactions to the shattering of hope vary a great deal, depending on many circumstances: historical, personal, psychological, and constitutional. Many people, probably the majority, react to the disappointment of their hopes by adjustment to the average optimism which hopes for the best without bothering to recognize that not even the good but perhaps, indeed, the worst may occur. As long as everybody else whistles, such people whistle too, and instead of feeling their hopelessness, they seem to participate in a kind of pop concert. They reduce their demands to what they can get and do not even dream of that which seems to be out of their reach. They are well-adjusted members of the herd and they never feel hopeless because nobody else seems to feel hopeless. They present the picture of a peculiar kind of resigned optimism which we see in so many members of contemporary Western society—the optimism usually being conscious and the resignation unconscious.

Another outcome of the shattering of hope is the "hardening of the heart." We see many people—from juvenile delinquents to hard-boiled but effective adults —who at one point of their lives, maybe at five, maybe at twelve, maybe at twenty, cannot stand to be hurt any more. Some of them, as in a sudden vision or conversion, decide that they have had enough; that they will not feel anything any more; that nobody will ever be able to hurt them, but that they will be able to hurt others. They may complain about their bad luck in not finding any friends or anyone who loves them, but it is not their bad luck, it is their fate. Having lost compassion and empathy, they do not touch anybody—nor can they be touched. Their triumph in life is not to need anybody. They take pride in their untouchability and pleasure in being able to hurt. Whether this is done in criminal or legitimate ways depends much more on social factors than on psychological ones. Most of them remain frozen and hence unhappy until their lives run out. Not so rarely, a miracle happens and a thaw begins. It may simply be that they meet a person in whose concern or interest they believe, and new dimensions of feeling open. If they are lucky, they unfreeze completely and the seeds of hope which seem to have been destroyed altogether come to life.

Another and much more drastic result of shattered hope is destructiveness and violence. Precisely because men cannot live without hope, the one whose hope has been utterly destroyed hates life. Since he cannot create life, he wants to destroy it, which is only a little less of a miracle—but much more easy to accomplish. He wants to avenge himself for his unlived life and he does it by throwing himself into total destructiveness so that it matters little whether he destroys others or is destroyed.[14]

Usually the destructive reaction to shattered hope is to be found among those who, for social or economic reasons, are excluded from the comforts of the majority and have no place to go socially or economically. It is not primarily the economic frustration which leads to hate and violence; it is the hopelessness of the situation,

---

[14] This problem and that of other manifestations of destructiveness are dealt with in detail in my forthcoming book, *The Causes of Human Destructiveness.*

the ever-repeated broken promises, which are just as conducive to violence and destructiveness. In fact, there is little doubt that groups which are so deprived and mistreated that they cannot even be hopeless because they have no vision of hope are less violent than those who see the possibility of hope and yet recognize at the same time that the circumstances make the realization of their hopes impossible. Psychologically speaking, destructiveness is the alternative to hope, just as attraction to death is the alternative to the love of life, and just as joy is the alternative to boredom.

Not only does the individual live by hope. Nations and social classes live through hope, faith, and fortitude, and if they lose this potential they disappear—either by their lack of vitality or by the irrational destructiveness which they develop.

Note should be taken of the fact that the development of hope or hopelessness in an individual is largely determined by the presence of hope or hopelessness in his society or class. However shattered an individual's hope may have been in childhood, if he lives in a period of hope and faith, his own hope will be kindled; on the other hand, the person whose experience leads him to be hopeful will often tend to be depressed and hopeless when his society or class has lost the spirit of hope.

Today, and increasingly so since the beginning of the First World War, and perhaps specifically in America ever since the defeat of the Anti-Imperialist League at the end of the last century, hope is disappearing fast in the Western world. As I said before, the hopelessness is covered up as optimism and, in a few, as revolutionary nihilism. But whatever a man thinks about himself is of little importance in comparison with what he is, with what he truly feels, and most of us are not aware of what we feel.

The signs of hopelessness are all here. Look at the bored expression of the average person, the lack of contact between people—even when they desperately try "to make contact." Look at the incapacity to plan seri-

ously for overcoming the ever-increasing poisonousness
of the city's water and air and the predictable famine in
the poor countries, not to speak of the inability to get
rid of the daily threat to the lives and plans of all of us
—the thermonuclear weapon. Whatever we say or think
about hope, our inability to act or plan for life betrays
our hopelessness.

We know a little about the reasons for this growing
hopelessness. Before 1914 people thought that the
world was a safe place, that wars, with their complete
disregard for human life, were a matter of the past. And
yet, the First World War took place and every government lied about its motives. Then came the Spanish
Civil War, with its comedy of pretensions both from the
Western powers and from the Soviet Union; the terror of
the Stalin system and the Hitler system; the Second
World War, with its complete disregard for the lives of
civilians; and the war in Vietnam, where for years the
American government has tried to use its power to crush
a small people in order to "save it." And neither one
of the great powers has made the one step which would
have given hope to all: getting rid of its own nuclear
weapons, trusting the sanity of the others to be sane
enough to follow suit.

But there are still other reasons for the increasing
hopelessness: the formation of the totally bureaucra-
tized industrial society and the powerlessness of the individual vis-à-vis the organization, which I shall deal with
in the next chapter.

If America and the Western world continue in their
state of unconscious hopelessness, lack of faith and of
fortitude, it is predictable that they will not be able to
resist the temptation of the big bang by nuclear weapons,
which would end all problems—overpopulation, boredom, and hunger—since it would do away with all life.

Progress in the direction of a social and cultural order
in which man is in the saddle depends on our capacity to
come to grips with our hopelessness. First of all, we have
to see it. And second, we have to examine whether there

is a real possibility of changing our social, economic, and cultural life in a new direction which will make it possible to hope again. If there is no such real possibility, then indeed hope is sheer foolishness. But if there is a real possibility, there can be hope, based on examination of new alternatives and options, and on concerted actions to bring about the realization of these new alternatives.

Chapter III

Where Are We Now and
Where Are We Headed?

1. WHERE ARE WE NOW?

It is difficult to locate our exact position on the historical trajectory leading from eighteenth- and nineteenth-century industrialism to the future. It is easier to say where we are *not*. We are not on the way to free enterprise, but are moving rapidly away from it. We are not on the way to greater individualism, but are becoming an increasingly manipulated mass civilization. We are not on the way to the places toward which our ideological maps tell us we are moving. We are marching in an entirely different direction. Some see the direction quite clearly; among them are those who favor it and those who fear it. But most of us look at maps which are as different from reality as was the map of the world in the year 500 B.C. It is not enough to know that our maps are false. It is important to have correct maps if we are to be able to go in the direction we want to go. The most important feature of the new map is the indication that we have passed the stage of the first Industrial Revolution and have begun the period of the second Industrial Revolution.

The first Industrial Revolution was characterized by the fact that man had learned to replace live energy (that of animals and men) by mechanical energy (that of steam, oil, electricity, and the atom). These new sources of energy were the basis for a fundamental change in industrial production. Related to this new industrial potential was a certain type of industrial organization, that of a great number of what we would call today small or medium-sized industrial enterprises, which were managed by their owners, which competed with each other, and which exploited their workers and fought with them about the share of the profits. The member of the middle and upper class was the master of his enterprise, as he was the master of his home, and he considered himself to be the master of his destiny. Ruthless exploitation of nonwhite populations went together with domestic reform, increasingly benevolent attitudes toward the poor, and eventually, in the first half of this century, the rise of the working class from abysmal poverty to a relatively comfortable life.

The first Industrial Revolution is being followed by the second Industrial Revolution, the beginning of which we witness at the present time. It is characterized by the fact not only that *living energy* has been replaced by mechanical energy, but that *human thought* is being replaced by the thinking of machines. Cybernetics and automation ("cybernation") make it possible to build machines that function much more precisely and much more quickly than the human brain for the purpose of answering important technical and organizational questions. Cybernation is creating the possibility of a new kind of economic and social organization. A relatively small number of mammoth enterprises has become the center of the economic machine and will rule it completely in the not-too-distant future. The enterprise, although legally the property of hundreds of thousands of stockholders, is managed (and for all practical purposes managed independently of the legal owners) by a self-perpetuating bureaucracy. The alliance between private business and government is becoming so close that the two components of this alliance become ever less distinguishable. The majority of the population in America is well fed, well housed, and well amused, and the sector of "underdeveloped" Americans who still live under substandard conditions will probably join the

majority in the foreseeable future. We continue to pro-
fess individualism, freedom, and faith in God, but our
professions are wearing thin when compared with the
reality of the organization man's obsessional conformity
guided by the principle of hedonistic materialism.

If society could stand still—which it can do as little
as an individual—things might not be as ominous as
they are. But we are headed in the direction of a new
kind of society and a new kind of human life, of which
we now see only the beginning and which is rapidly ac-
celerating.

2. THE VISION OF THE DEHUMANIZED SOCIETY OF A.D. 2000

What is the kind of society and the kind of man we
might find in the year 2000, provided nuclear war has
not destroyed the human race before then?

If people knew the likely course which American
society will take, many if not most of them would be so
horrified that they might take adequate measures to permit changing the course. If people are not aware of the
direction in which they are going, they will awaken when
it is too late and when their fate has been irrevocably
sealed. Unfortunately, the vast majority are not aware
of where they are going. They are not aware that the
new society toward which they are moving is as radically
different from Greek and Roman, medieval and traditional industrial societies as the agricultural society
was from that of the food gatherers and hunters. Most
people still think in the concepts of the society of the
first Industrial Revolution. They see that we have more
and better machines than man had fifty years ago and
mark this down as progress. They believe that lack of
direct political oppression is a manifestation of the
achievement of personal freedom. Their vision of the
year 2000 is that it will be the full realization of the

aspirations of man since the end of the Middle Ages, and they do not see that the year 2000 may be not the fulfillment and happy culmination of a period in which man struggled for freedom and happiness, but the beginning of a period in which man ceases to be human and becomes transformed into an unthinking and unfeeling machine.

It is interesting to note that the dangers of the new dehumanized society were already clearly recognized by intuitive minds in the nineteenth century, and it adds to the impressiveness of their vision that they were people of opposite political camps.[1]

A conservative like Disraeli and a socialist like Marx were practically of the same opinion concerning the danger to man that would arise from the uncontrolled growth of production and consumption. They both saw how man would become weakened by enslavement to the machine and his own ever increasing cupidity. Disraeli thought the solution could be found by containing the power of the new bourgeoisie; Marx believed that a highly industrialized society could be transformed into a humane one, in which man and not material goods were the goal of all social efforts.[2] One of the most brilliant progressive thinkers of the last century, John Stuart Mill, saw the problem with all clarity:

> I confess I am not charmed with the ideal of life held out by those who think that the normal state of human beings is that of struggling to get on; that the trampling, crushing, elbowing, and treading on each other's heels, which form the existing type of social life, are the most desirable lot of human kind, or anything but the disagreeable symptoms of one of the phases of industrial progress. . . . Most fitting, indeed, is it, that while riches are power, and to

---

[1] Cf. the statements of Burckhardt, Proudhon, Baudelaire, Thoreau, Marx, Tolstoy quoted in *The Sane Society*, pp. 184 ff.

[2] Cf. Erich Fromm, *Marx's Concept of Man* (New York: Ungar, 1961).

grow as rich as possible the universal object of ambition, the path to its attainment should be open to all, without favour or partiality. But the best state for human nature is that in which, while no one is poor, no one desires to be richer, nor has any reason to fear being thrust back by the efforts of others to push themselves forward.[3]

It seems that great minds a hundred years ago saw what would happen today or tomorrow, while we to whom it is happening blind ourselves in order not to be disturbed in our daily routine. It seems that liberals and conservatives are equally blind in this respect. There are only few writers of vision who have clearly seen the monster to which we are giving birth. It is not Hobbes' *Leviathan*, but a Moloch, the all-destructive idol, to which human life is to be sacrificed. This Moloch has been described most imaginatively by Orwell and Aldous Huxley, by a number of science-fiction writers who show more perspicacity than most professional sociologists and psychologists.

I have already quoted Brzezinski's description of the technetronic society, and only want to quote the following addition: "The largely humanist-oriented, occasionally ideologically-minded intellectual-dissenter . . . is rapidly being displaced either by experts and specialists . . . or by the generalists-integrators, who become in effect house-ideologues for those in power, providing overall intellectual integration for disparate actions." [4]

A profound and brilliant picture of the new society has been given recently by one of the most outstanding humanists of our age, Lewis Mumford.[5] Future historians, if there are any, will consider his work to be one of the prophetic warnings of our time. Mumford gives new depth and perspective to the future by analyzing its

---

[3] *Principles of Political Economy* (London: Longmans, 1929; 1st Edition, 1848).

[4] "The Technetronic Society," p. 19.

[5] Lewis Mumford, *The Myth of the Machine.*

roots in the past. The central phenomenon which connects past and future, as he sees it, he calls the "megamachine."

The "megamachine" is the totally organized and homogenized social system in which society as such functions like a machine and men like its parts. This kind of organization by total coordination, by "the constant increase of order, power, predictability and above all control," achieved almost miraculous technical results in early megamachines like the Egyptian and Mesopotamian societies, and it will find its fullest expression, with the help of modern technology, in the future of the technological society.

Mumford's concept of the megamachine helps to make clear certain recent phenomena. The first time the megamachine was used on a large scale in modern times was, it seems to me, in the Stalinist system of industrialization, and after that, in the system used by Chinese Communism. While Lenin and Trotsky still hoped that the Revolution would eventually lead to the mastery of society by the individual, as Marx had visualized, Stalin betrayed whatever was left of these hopes and sealed the betrayal by the physical extinction of all those in whom the hope might not have completely disappeared. Stalin could build his megamachine on the nucleus of a well-developed industrial sector, even though one far below those of countries like England or the United States. The Communist leaders in China were confronted with a different situation. They had no industrial nucleus to speak of. Their only capital was the physical energy and the passions and thoughts of 700 million people. They decided that by means of the complete coordination of this human material they could create the equivalent of the original accumulation of capital necessary to achieve a technical development which in a relatively short time would reach the level of that of the West. This total coordination had to be achieved by a mixture of force, personality cult, and indoctrination which is in contrast to the freedom and individualism Marx had foreseen as the essential elements of a socialist society. One must not forget, however, that the ideals of the overcoming of private egotism and of maximal consumption have remained elements in the Chinese system, at least thus far, although blended with totalitarianism, nationalism, and thought control, thus vitiating the humanist vision of Marx.

The insight into this radical break between the first phase of industrialization and the second Industrial Revolution, in which society itself becomes a vast machine, of which man is a living particle, is obscured by certain important differences between the megamachine of Egypt and that of the twentieth century. First of all, the labor of the live parts of the Egyptian machine was forced labor. The naked threat of death or starvation forced the Egyptian worker to carry out his task. Today, in the twentieth century, the worker in the most developed industrial countries, such as the United States, has a comfortable life—one which would have seemed like a life of undreamed-of luxury to his ancestor working a hundred years ago. He has, and in this point lies one of the errors of Marx, participated in the economic progress of capitalist society, profited from it, and, indeed, has a great deal more to lose than his chains.

The bureaucracy which directs the work is very different from the bureaucratic elite of the old megamachine. Its life is guided more or less by the same middle-class virtues that are valid for the worker; although its members are better paid than the worker, the difference in consumption is one of quantity rather than quality. Employers and workers smoke the same cigarettes and they ride in cars that look the same even though the better cars run more smoothly than the cheaper ones. They watch the same movies and the same television shows, and their wives use the same refrigerators.[6]

---

[6] The fact that the underdeveloped sector of the population does not take part in this new style of life has been mentioned above.

The managerial elite are also different from those of old in another respect: they are just as much appendages of the machine as those whom they command. They are just as alienated, or perhaps more so, just as anxious, or perhaps more so, as the worker in one of their factories. They are bored, like everyone else, and use the same antidotes against boredom. They are not as the elites were of old—a culture-creating group. Although they spend a good deal of their money to further science and art, as a class they are as much consumers of this "cultural welfare" as its recipients. The culture-creating group lives on the fringes. They are creative scientists and artists, but it seems that, thus far, the most beautiful blossom of twentieth-century society grows on the tree of science, and not on the tree of art.

3. THE PRESENT TECHNOLOGICAL SOCIETY

a. Its Principles

The technetronic society may be the system of the future, but it is not yet here; it can develop from what is already here, and it probably will, unless a sufficient number of people see the danger and redirect our course. In order to do so, it is necessary to understand in greater detail the operation of the present technological system and the effect it has on man.

What are the guiding principles of this system as it is today?

It is programed by two principles that direct the efforts and thoughts of everyone working in it: The first principle is the maxim that something *ought* to be done because it is technically *possible* to do it. If it is possible to build nuclear weapons, they must be built even if they might destroy us all. If it is possible to travel to the moon or to the planets, it must be done, even if at the expense of many unfulfilled needs here on earth. This principle means the negation of all values which the humanist tradition has developed. This tradi-

tion said that something should be done because it is
needed for man, for his growth, joy, and reason, because
it is beautiful, good, or true. Once the principle is accepted that something ought to be done because it is
technically possible to do it, all other values are de-
throned, and technological development becomes the
foundation of ethics.[7]

The second principle is that of *maximal efficiency and
output*. The requirement of maximal efficiency leads as
a consequence to the requirement of minimal individuality. The social machine works more efficiently, so it is
believed, if individuals are cut down to purely quantifi-
able units whose personalities can be expressed on
punched cards. These units can be administered more
easily by bureaucratic rules because they do not make
trouble or create friction. In order to reach this result,
men must be de-individualized and taught to find their
identity in the corporation rather than in themselves.

The question of economic efficiency requires careful
thought. The issue of being economically efficient, that
is to say, using the smallest possible amount of resources
to obtain maximal effect, should be placed in a historical and evolutionary context. The question is obviously
more important in a society where real material scarcity

---

[7] While revising this manuscript I read a paper by Hasan
Ozbekhan, "The Triumph of Technology: 'Can' Implies
'Ought.'" This paper, adapted from an invited presentation at
MIT and published in mimeographed form by System Development Corporation, Santa Monica, California, was sent to me by
the courtesy of Mr. George Weinwurm. As the title indicates,
Ozbekhan expresses the same concept as the one I present in
the text. His is a brilliant presentation of the problem from the
standpoint of an outstanding specialist in the field of management science, and I find it a very encouraging fact that the same
idea appears in the work of authors in fields as different as his
and mine. I quote a sentence that shows the identity of his concept and the one presented in the text: "Thus, feasibility, which
is a strategic concept, becomes elevated into a normative concept, with the result that whatever technological reality indicates
we *can* do is taken as implying that we *must* do it" (p. 7).

is the prime fact of life, and its importance diminishes as the productive powers of a society advance.

A second line of investigation should be a full consideration of the fact that efficiency is only a known element in already existing activities. Since we do not know much about the efficiency or inefficiency of untried approaches, one must be careful in pleading for things as they are on the grounds of efficiency. Furthermore, one must be very careful to think through and specify the area and time period being examined. What may appear efficient by a narrow definition can be highly inefficient if the time and scope of the discussion are broadened. In economics there is increasing awareness of what are called "neighborhood effects"; that is, effects that go beyond the immediate activity and are often neglected in considering benefits and costs. One example would be evaluating the efficiency of a particular industrial project only in terms of the immediate effects on this enterprise—forgetting, for instance, that waste materials deposited in nearby streams and the air represent a costly and a serious inefficiency with regard to the community. We need to clearly develop standards of efficiency that take account of time and society's interest as a whole. Eventually, the human element needs to be taken into account as a basic factor in the system whose efficiency we try to examine.

Dehumanization in the name of efficiency is an all-too-common occurrence; e.g., giant telephone systems employing Brave New World techniques of recording operators' contacts with customers and asking customers to evaluate workers' performance and attitudes, etc.—all aimed at instilling "proper" employee attitude, standardizing service, and increasing efficiency. From the narrow perspective of immediate company purposes, this may yield docile, manageable workers, and thus enhance company efficiency. In terms of the employees, as human beings, the effect is to engender feelings of inadequacy, anxiety, and frustration, which may lead to either indifference or hostility. In broader terms, even efficiency may not be served, since the company and society at large doubtless pay a heavy price for these practices.

Another general practice in organizing work is to constantly remove elements of creativity (involving an element of risk or uncertainty) and group work by dividing and subdividing tasks to the point where no judgment or interpersonal contact remains or is required. Workers and technicians are by no means insensitive to this process. Their frustration is often perceptive and articulate, and comments such as "We are human" and "The work is not fit for human beings" are not uncommon. Again, efficiency in a narrow sense can be demoralizing and costly in individual and social terms.

If we are only concerned with input-output figures, a system may give the impression of efficiency. If we take into account what the given methods do to the human beings in the system, we may discover that they are bored, anxious, depressed, tense, etc. The result would be a twofold one: (1) Their imagination would be hobbled by their psychic pathology, they would be uncreative, their thinking would be routinized and bureaucratic, and hence they would not come up with new ideas and solutions which would contribute to a more productive development of the system; altogether, their energy would be considerably lowered. (2) They would suffer from many physical ills, which are the result of stress and tension; this loss in health is also a loss for the system. Furthermore, if one examines what this tension and anxiety do to them in their relationship to their wives and children, and in their functioning as responsible citizens, it may turn out that for the system as a whole the seemingly efficient method is most inefficient, not only in human terms but also as measured by merely economic criteria.

To sum up: efficiency is desirable in any kind of purposeful activity. But it should be examined in terms of the larger systems, of which the system under study is only a part; it should take account of the human factor within the system. Eventually efficiency as such should not be a *dominant* norm in any kind of enterprise.

The other aspect of the same principle, that of *maximum output,* formulated very simply, maintains that the more we produce of whatever we produce, the better. The success of the economy of the country is measured by its rise of total production. So is the success of a company. Ford may lose several hundred million dollars by the failure of a costly new model, like the Edsel, but this is only a minor mishap as long as the production curve rises. The growth of the economy is visualized in terms of ever-increasing production, and there is no vision of a limit yet where production may be stabilized. The comparison between countries rests upon the same principle. The Soviet Union hopes to surpass the United States by accomplishing a more rapid rise in economic growth.

Not only industrial production is ruled by the principle of continuous and limitless acceleration. The educational system has the same criterion: the more college graduates, the better. The same in sports: every new record is looked upon as progress. Even the attitude toward the weather seems to be determined by the same principle. It is emphasized that this is "the hottest day in the decade," or the coldest, as the case may be, and I suppose some people are comforted for the inconvenience by the proud feeling that they are witnesses to the record temperature. One could go on endlessly giving examples of the concept that constant increase of quantity constitutes the goal of our life; in fact, that it is what is meant by "progress."

Few people raise the question of *quality,* or what all this increase in quantity is good for. This omission is evident in a society which is not centered around man any more, in which one aspect, that of quantity, has choked all others. It is easy to see that the predominance of this principle of "the more the better" leads to an imbalance in the whole system. If all efforts are bent on doing *more*, the quality of living loses all importance, and activities that once were means become ends.[8]

If the overriding economic principle is that we produce more and more, the consumer must be prepared to want—that is, to consume—more and more. Industry does not rely on the consumer's spontaneous desires for more and more commodities. By building in obsolescence it often forces him to buy new things when the old ones could last much longer. By changes in styling of products, dresses, durable goods, and even food, it forces him psychologically to buy more than he might need or want. But industry, in its need for increased production, does not rely on the consumer's needs and wants but to a considerable extent on advertising, which

---

[8] I find in C. West Churchman's *Challenge to Reason* (New York: McGraw-Hill, 1968) an excellent formulation of the problem:

"If we explore this idea of a larger and larger model of systems, we may be able to see in what sense completeness represents a challenge to reason. One model that seems to be a good candidate for completeness is called an *allocation* model; it views the world as a system of activities that use resources to 'output' usable products.

"The process of reasoning in this model is very simple. One searches for a central quantitative measure of system performance, which has the characteristic: the more of this quantity the better. For example, the more profit a firm makes, the better. The more qualified students a university graduates, the better. The more food we produce, the better. It will turn out that the particular choice of the measure of system performance is not critical, so long as it is a measure of general concern.

"We take this desirable measure of performance and relate it to the feasible activities of the system. The activities may be the operations of various manufacturing plants, of schools and universities, of farms, and so on. Each significant activity contributes to the desirable quantity in some recognizable way. The contribution, in fact, can often be expressed in a mathematical function that maps the amount of activity onto the amount of the desirable quantity. The more sales of a certain product, the higher the profit of a firm. The more courses we teach, the more graduates we have. The more fertilizer we use, the more food" (pp. 156–57).

is the most important offensive against the consumer's right to know what he wants. The spending of 16.5 billion dollars on direct advertising in 1966 (in newspapers, magazines, radio, TV) may sound like an irrational and wasteful use of human talents, of paper and print. But it is not irrational in a system that believes that increasing production and hence consumption is a vital feature of our economic system, without which it would collapse. If we add to the cost of advertising the considerable cost for restyling of durable goods, especially cars, and of packaging, which partly is another form of whetting the consumer's appetite, it is clear that industry is willing to pay a high price for the guarantee of the upward production and sales curve.[9]

The anxiety of industry about what might happen to our economy if our style of life changed is expressed in this brief quote by a leading investment banker:

> Clothing would be purchased for its utility; food would be bought on the basis of economy and nutritional value; automobiles would be stripped to essentials and held by the same owners for the full 10 to 15 years of their useful lives; homes would be built and maintained for their characteristics of shelter, without regard to style or neighborhood. And what would happen to a market dependent upon new models, new styles, new ideas? [10]

b. Its Effect on Man

What is the effect of this type of organization on man? It reduces man to an appendage of the machine, ruled by its very rhythm and demands. It transforms him into *Homo consumens,* the total consumer, whose only aim

---

[9] The problem of whether the unlimited rise in production and consumption is an economic necessity will be discussed in Chapter V.

[10] Paul Mazur, *The Standards We Raise,* New York, 1953, p. 32.

is to *have* more and to *use* more. This society produces many useless things, and to the same degree many useless people. Man, as a cog in the production machine, becomes a thing, and ceases to be human. He spends his time doing things in which he is not interested, with people in whom he is not interested, producing things in which he is not interested; and when he is not producing, he is consuming. He is the eternal suckling with the open mouth, "taking in," without effort and without inner activeness, whatever the boredom-preventing (and boredom-producing) industry forces on him—cigarettes, liquor, movies, television, sports, lectures—limited only by what he can afford. But the boredom-preventing industry, that is to say, the gadget-selling industry, the automobile industry, the movie industry, the television industry, and so on, can only succeed in preventing the boredom from becoming conscious. In fact, they increase the boredom, as a salty drink taken to quench the thirst increases it. However unconscious, boredom remains boredom nevertheless.

The passiveness of man in industrial society today is one of his most characteristic and pathological features. He takes in, he wants to be fed, but he does not move, initiate, he does not digest his food, as it were. He does not reacquire in a productive fashion what he inherited, but he amasses it or consumes it. He suffers from a severe systemic deficiency, not too dissimilar to that which one finds in more extreme forms in depressed people.

Man's passiveness is only one symptom among a total syndrome, which one may call the "syndrome of alienation." Being passive, he does not relate himself to the world actively and is forced to submit to his idols and their demands. Hence, he feels powerless, lonely, and anxious. He has little sense of integrity or self-identity. Conformity seems to be the only way to avoid intolerable anxiety—and even conformity does not always alleviate his anxiety.

No American writer has perceived this dynamism more clearly than Thorstein Veblen. He wrote:

> In all the received formulations of economic theory, whether at the hands of the English economists or those of the continent, the human material with which the inquiry is concerned is conceived in hedonistic terms; that is to say, in terms of a passive and substantially inert and immutably given human nature . . . The hedonistic conception of man is that of a lightning calculator of pleasures and pains, who oscillates like a homogeneous globule of desire of happiness under the impulse of stimuli that shift him about the area, but leave him intact. He has neither antecedent nor consequent. He is an isolated, definitive human datum, in stable equilibrium except for the buffets of the impinging forces that displace him in one direction or another. Self-imposed in elemental space, he spins symmetrically about his own spiritual axis until the parallelogram of forces bears down upon him, whereupon he follows the line of the resultant. When the force of the impact is spent, he comes to rest, a self-contained globule of desire as before. Spiritually, the hedonistic man is not a prime mover. *He is not the seat of a process of living, except in the sense that he is subject to a series of permutations enforced upon him by circumstances external and alien to him.*[11]

Aside from the pathological traits that are rooted in passiveness, there are others which are important for the understanding of today's pathology of normalcy. I am referring to the growing split of cerebral-intellectual function from affective-emotional experience; the split between thought from feeling, mind from the heart, truth from passion.

---

[11] "Why Is Economics Not an Evolutionary Science?," in *The Place of Science in Modern Civilization and Other Essays* (New York: B. W. Huebsch, 1919), p. 73. (Emphasis added.)

Logical thought is not rational if it is merely logical [12] and not guided by the concern for life, and by the inquiry into the total process of living in all its concreteness and with all its contradictions. On the other hand, not only thinking but also emotions can be rational. *"Le coeur a ses raisons que la raison ne connaît point,"* as Pascal put it. (The heart has its reasons which reason knows nothing of.) Rationality in emotional life means that the emotions affirm and help the person's psychic structure to maintain a harmonious balance and at the same time to assist its growth. Thus, for instance, irrational love is love which enhances the person's dependency, hence anxiety and hostility. Rational love is a love which relates a person intimately to another, at the same time preserving his independence and integrity.

Reason flows from the blending of rational thought and feeling. If the two functions are torn apart, thinking deteriorates into schizoid intellectual activity, and feeling deteriorates into neurotic life-damaging passions.

The split between thought and affect leads to a sickness, to a low-grade chronic schizophrenia, from which the new man of the technetronic age begins to suffer. In the social sciences it has become fashionable to think about human problems with no reference to the feelings related to these problems. It is assumed that scientific objectivity demands that thoughts and theories concerning man be emptied of all emotional concern with man.

An example of this emotion-free thinking is Herman Kahn's book on thermonuclear warfare. The question is discussed: how many millions of dead Americans are "acceptable" if we use as a criterion the ability to rebuild the economic machine after nuclear war in a reasonably short time so that it is as good as or better than before. Figures for GNP and population increase

---

[12] Paranoid thinking is characterized by the fact that it can be completely logical, yet lack any guidance by concern or concrete inquiry into reality; in other words, logic does not exclude madness.

or decrease are the basic categories in this kind of thinking, while the question of the human results of nuclear war in terms of suffering, pain, brutalization, etc., is left aside.

Kahn's *The Year 2000* is another example of the writing which we may expect in the completely alienated megamachine society. Kahn's concern is that of the figures for production, population increase, and various scenarios for war or peace, as the case may be. He impresses many readers because they mistake the thousands of little data which he combines in ever-changing kaleidoscopic pictures for erudition or profundity. They do not notice the basic superficiality in his reasoning and the lack of the human dimension in his description of the future.

When I speak here of low-grade chronic schizophrenia, a brief explanation seems to be needed. Schizophrenia, like any other psychotic state, must be defined not only in psychiatric terms but also in social terms. Schizophrenic experience *beyond* a certain threshold would be considered a sickness in any society, since those suffering from it would be unable to function under any social circumstances (unless the schizophrenic is elevated into the status of a god, shaman, saint, priest, etc.). But there are low-grade chronic forms of psychoses which can be shared by millions of people and which—precisely because they do not go beyond a certain threshold—do not prevent these people from functioning socially. As long as they share their sickness with millions of others, they have the satisfactory feeling of not being alone; in other words, they avoid that sense of complete isolation which is so characteristic of full-fledged psychosis. On the contrary, they look at themselves as normal and at those who have not lost the link between heart and mind as being "crazy." In all low-grade forms of psychoses, the definition of sickness depends on the question as to whether the pathology is shared or not. Just as there is low-grade chronic schizophrenia, so there exist also low-grade chonic paranoia and depression. And there is plenty of evidence that among certain strata of the population, particularly on occasions where a war threatens, the paranoid elements increase but are not felt as pathological as long as they are common.[13]

The tendency to install technical progress as the highest value is linked up not only with our overemphasis on intellect but, most importantly, with a deep emotional attraction to the mechanical, to all that is not alive, to all that is man-made. This attraction to the non-alive, which is in its more extreme form an attraction to death and decay (necrophilia), leads even in its less drastic form to indifference toward life instead of "reverence for life." Those who are attracted to the non-alive are the people who prefer "law and order" to living structure, bureaucratic to spontaneous methods, gadgets to living beings, repetition to originality, neatness to exuberance, hoarding to spending. They want to control life because they are afraid of its uncontrollable spontaneity; they would rather kill it than to expose themselves to it and merge with the world around them. They often gamble with death because they are not rooted in life; their courage is the courage to die and the symbol of their ultimate courage is the Russian

---

[13] The difference between that which is considered to be sickness and that which is considered to be normal becomes apparent in the following example. If a man declared that in order to free our cities from air pollution, factories, automobiles, airplanes, etc., would have to be destroyed, nobody would doubt that he was insane. But if there is a consensus that in order to protect our life, our freedom, our culture, or that of other nations which we feel obliged to protect, thermonuclear war might be required as a last resort, such opinion appears to be perfectly sane. The difference is not at all in the kind of thinking employed but merely in that the first idea is not shared and hence appears abnormal while the second is shared by millions of people and by powerful governments and hence appears to be normal.

roulette.[14] The rate of our automobile accidents and the preparation for thermonuclear war are a testimony to this readiness to gamble with death. And who would not eventually prefer this exciting gamble to the boring unaliveness of the organization man?

One symptom of the attraction of the merely mechanical is the growing popularity, among some scientists and the public, of the idea that it will be possible to construct computers which are no different from man in thinking, feeling, or any other aspect of functioning.[15] The main problem, it seems to me, is not whether such a computer-man can be constructed; it is rather why the idea is becoming so popular in a historical period when nothing seems to be more important than to transform the existing man into a more rational, harmonious, and peace-loving being. One cannot help being suspicious that often the attraction of the computer-man idea is the expression of a flight from life and from humane experience into the mechanical and purely cerebral.

The possibility that we can build robots who are like men belongs, if anywhere, to the future. But the present already shows us men who act like robots. When the majority of men are like robots, then indeed there will be no problem in building robots who are like men. The idea of the manlike computer is a good example of the alternative between the human and the

---

[14] Michael Maccoby has demonstrated the incidence of the life-loving versus the death-loving syndrome in various populations by the application of an "interpretative" questionnaire. Cf. his "Polling Emotional Attitudes in Relation to Political Choices" (to be published).

[15] Dean E. Wooldridge, for instance, in *Mechanical Man* (New York: McGraw-Hill, 1968), writes that it will be possible to manufacture computers synthetically which are "completely undistinguishable from human beings produced in the usual manner" [!] (p. 172). Marvin L. Minsky, a great authority on computers, writes in his book *Computation* (Englewood Cliffs, N.J.: Prentice-Hall, 1967): "There is no reason to suppose machines have any limitations not shared by man" (p. vii).

inhuman use of machines. The computer can serve the enhancement of life in many respects. But the idea that it replaces man and life is the manifestation of the pathology of today.

The fascination with the merely mechanical is supplemented by an increasing popularity of conceptions that stress the animal nature of man and the instinctive roots of his emotions or actions. Freud's was such an instinctive psychology; but the importance of his concept of libido is secondary in comparison with his fundamental discovery of the unconscious process in waking life or in sleep. The most popular recent authors who stress instinctual animal heredity, like Konrad Lorenz (*On Aggression*) or Desmond Morris (*The Naked Ape*), have not offered any new or valuable insights into the specific human problem as Freud has done; they satisfy the wish of many to look at themselves as determined by instincts and thus to camouflage their true and bothersome human problems.[16] The dream of many people seems to be to combine the emotions of a primate with a computerlike brain. If this dream could be fulfilled, the problem of human freedom and of responsibility would seem to disappear. Man's feelings would be determined by his instincts, his reason by the computer; man would not have to give an answer to the questions his existence asks him. Whether one likes the dream or not, its realization is impossible; the naked ape with the computer brain would cease to be human, or rather "he" would not *be*.[17]

Among the technological society's pathogenic effects

---

[16] This criticism of Lorenz refers only to that part of his work in which he deals by analogy with the psychological problems of man, not with his work in the field of animal behavior and instinct theory.

[17] In revising this manuscript I became aware that Lewis Mumford had expressed the same idea in 1954 in *In the Name on Socialist Humanism*, ed. Erich Fromm (New York: Double-

"Modern man, therefore, now approaches the last act of his tragedy, and I could not, even if I would, conceal its finality

upon man, two more must be mentioned: the disappearance of *privacy* and of *personal human contact*.

"Privacy" is a complex concept. It was and is a privilege of the middle and upper classes, since its very basis, private space, is costly. This privilege, however, can become a common good with other economic privileges. Aside from this economic factor, it was also based on a hoarding tendency in which *my* private life was *mine* and nobody else's, as was *my* house and any other property. It was also a concomitant of *cant,* of the discrepancy between moral appearances and reality. Yet when all these qualifications are made, privacy still seems to be an important condition for a person's productive development. First of all, because privacy is necessary to collect oneself and to free oneself from the constant "noise" of people's chatter and intrusion, which interferes with one's own mental processes. If all private data are transformed into public data, experiences will tend to become more shallow and more alike. People will be afraid to feel the "wrong thing"; they will become more accessible to psychological manipulation which, through psychological testing, tries to establish norms for "desirable," "normal," "healthy" attitudes. Considering that these tests are applied in order to help the companies and government agencies to find the people with the "best" attitudes, the use of psychological tests, which is by now an almost general condition for

---

or its horror. We have lived to witness the joining, in intimate partnership, of the automaton and the id, the id rising from the lower depths of the unconscious, and the automaton, the machine-like thinker and the manlike machine, wholly detached from other life-maintaining functions and human reactions, descending from the heights of conscious thought. The first force has proved more brutal, when released from the whole personality, than the most savage of beasts; the other force, so impervious to human emotions, human anxieties, human purposes, so committed to answering only the limited range of questions for which its apparatus was originally loaded, that it lacks the saving intelligence to turn off its own compulsive mechanism, even though it is pushing science as well as civilization to its own doom" [p. 198].

getting a good job, constitutes a severe infringement on the citizen's freedom. Unfortunately, a large number of psychologists devote whatever knowledge of man they have to this manipulation in the interests of what the big organization considers efficiency. Thus, psychologists become an important part of the industrial and governmental system while claiming that their activities serve the optimal development of man. This claim is based on the rationalization that what is best for the corporation is best for man. It is important that the managers understand that much of what they get from psychological testing is based on the very limited picture of man which, in fact, management requirements have transmitted to the psychologists, who in turn give it back to management, allegedly as a result of an independent study of man. It hardly needs to be said that the intrusion of privacy may lead to a control of the individual which is more total and could be more devastating than what totalitarian states have demonstrated thus far. Orwell's 1984 will need much assistance from testing, conditioning, and smoothing-out by psychologists in order to come true. It is of vital importance to distinguish between a psychology that understands and aims at the well-being of man and a psychology that studies man as an object, with the aim of making him more useful for the technological society.

c. The Need for Certainty

In our discussion thus far, I have omitted one factor of the greatest importance for the understanding of man's behavior in present society: man's need for *certainty*. Man is not equipped with a set of instincts that regulate his behavior quasi-automatically. He is confronted with choices, and this means in all-important matters with grave risks to his life if his choices are wrong. The doubt that besets him when he must decide —often quickly—causes painful tension and can even seriously endanger his capacity for quick decisions. As a consequence, man has an intense need for certainty; he wants to believe that there is no need to doubt that the method by which he makes his decisions is right. In fact, he would rather make the "wrong" decision and be sure about it than the "right" decision and be tormented with doubt about its validity. This is one of the psychological reasons for man's belief in idols and political leaders. They all take out doubt and risk from his decision making; this does not mean that there is not a risk for his life, freedom, etc., *after* the decision has been made, but that there is no risk that the *method* of his decision making was wrong.

For many centuries certainty was guaranteed by the concept of God. God, omniscient and omnipotent, had not only created the world but also announced the principles of human action about which there was no doubt. The church "interpreted" these principles in detail, and the individual, securing his place in the church by following its rules, was certain that, whatever happened, he was on the way to salvation and to eternal life in heaven.[18]

With the beginning of the scientific approach and the corrosion of religious certainty, man was forced into a new search for certainty. At first, science seemed to be capable of giving a new basis for certainty. This was so for the rational man of the last centuries. But with the increasing complexities of life, which lost all human proportions, with the growing feeling of individual

---

[18] In the Lutheran-Calvinistic branch of Christian theology, man was taught not to be afraid of the risk of using false criteria for his decision making in a paradoxical way. Luther, belittling man's freedom and the role of his good works, taught that the only decision man has to make is to surrender his will totally to God, and thus to be released of the risk of making decisions on the basis of his own knowledge and responsibility. In Calvin's concept, everything is predestined, and man's decision does not really matter; yet his success is a sign that he is one of the chosen. In *Escape from Freedom*, I have pointed out the despair and anxiety in which these doctrines were rooted.

powerlessness and isolation, the science-oriented man ceased to be a rational and independent man. He lost the courage to think for himself and to make decisions on the basis of his full intellectual and emotional commitment to life. He wanted to exchange the "uncertain certainty" which rational thought can give for an "absolute certainty": the alleged "scientific" certainty, based on predictability.

This certainty is guaranteed not by man's own unreliable knowledge and emotions but by the computers which permit prediction and become guarantors of certainty. Take as an example the planning of the big corporation. With the help of computers, it can plan ahead for many years (including the manipulation of man's mind and taste); the manager does not have to rely any more on his individual judgment, but on the "truth" that is pronounced by the computers. The manager's decision may be wrong in its results, but he need not be distrustful of the decision-making processes. He feels that he is free to accept or reject the result of computer prognostication, but for all practical purposes, he is as little free as a pious Christian was to act against God's will. He could do it, but he would have to be out of his mind to take the risk, since there is not a greater source of certainty than God—or the computerized solution.

This need for certainty creates the need of what amounts to blind belief in the efficacy of the method of computerized planning. The managers are relieved from doubt, and so are those who are employed in the organization. It is precisely the fact that man's judgment and emotions allegedly do *not* interfere with the process of decision making that gives the computer-based planning its godlike quality.[19]

---

[19] Cf. the discussion of individual goals in decision making in Peer Soelberg, *Structure of Individual Goals: Implication for Organization Theory, the Psychology of Management Decision,* edited by George Fisk (Lund, Sweden: C. W. K. Gleerup, 1967), pp. 15–32.

In government policy and strategy, the same planning system becomes increasingly popular. The ideal is that foreign policy—and that means today also military planning—are freed from the arbitrariness of the human will and entrusted to a computer system, which tells the "truth" since it is not fallible like men, nor has it any ax to grind. The ideal is that all foreign policy and military strategy are based on computer decision, and this implies that all the facts are known, considered, and made available to the computer. With this method, doubt becomes excluded, although disaster is by no means necessarily avoided. But if disaster does happen after the decisions are made on the basis of unquestionable "facts," it is like an act of God, which one must accept, since man cannot do more than make the best decision he knows how to make.

It seems to me that these considerations are the only terms in which one can answer this puzzling question: How is it possible for our policy and strategy planners to tolerate the idea that at a certain point they may give orders the consequence of which will mean the destruction of their own families, most of America, and "at best" most of the industrialized world? If they rely on the decision the facts seem to have made *for them,* their conscience is cleared. However dreadful the consequences of their decisions may be, they need not have qualms about the rightness and legitimacy of the method by which they arrived at their decision. They act on faith, not essentially different from the faith on which the actions of the inquisitors of the Holy Office were based. Like Dostoevski's Grand Inquisitor, some may even be tragic figures who cannot act differently, because they see no other way of being certain that they do the best they can. The alleged rational character of our planners is basically not different from the religiously based decisions in a prescientific age. There is one qualification that must be made: both the religious decision, which is a blind surrender to God's will and the computer decision, based on the faith in the logic of "facts," are forms of alienated decisions in which man surrenders his own insight, knowledge, inquiry, and responsibility to an idol, be it God or the computer. The humanist religion of the prophets knew no such surrender; the decision was man's. He had to understand his situation, see the alternatives, and then decide. True scientific rationality is not different. The computer can help man in visualizing several possibilities, but the decision is not made for him, not only in the sense that he can choose between the various models, but also in the sense that he must use his reason, relate to and respond to the reality with which he deals, and elicit from the computer those facts which are relevant from the standpoint of reason, and that means from the standpoint of sustaining and fulfilling man's aliveness.

The blind and irrational reliance on computer decision becomes dangerous in foreign policy as well as strategic planning when done by opponents, each of whom works with his own data-processing system. He anticipates the opponent's moves, plans his own, and constructs scenarios for the X possibilities of moves on both sides. He can construct his game in many ways: that of his side winning, a stalemate, or both losing. But as Harvey Wheeler has pointed out,[20] if either "wins" it is the end of both. While the purpose of the game is to achieve a stalemate, the rules of the game make a stalemate unlikely. Both players, by their methods and their need for certainty, give up the way which has been that of precomputer diplomacy and strategy: the dialogue—with its possibility of give and take, open or veiled withdrawal, compromise, or even surrender when that is the only rational decision. With the present method, the dialogue, with all its possibilities for avoiding catastrophe, is ruled out. The action of the leaders is fanatical because it is pursued even to the point of self-destruction, although in a psychological sense they are not

---

[20] In *Unless Peace Comes,* edited by Nigel Calder (New York: The Viking Press, 1968), pp. 91 ff.

fanatics, because their actions are based on an emotion-free belief in the rationality (calculability) of the computer methods.

The hot line between Washington and Moscow is an ironical comment on this method of impersonal decision making. When the computer method seems to have set the two powers on a collision course, from which neither might be able to extricate himself, both sides employ the old-fashioned device of personal communication as the ultima ratio of political procedure. The Cuban missile crisis was solved with the help of a number of personal communications between Kennedy and Khrushchev. In 1967, at the time of the Arab-Israeli War, something similar happened. The Israeli attack on the American intelligence ship *Liberty* led to unusual American air-craft-based air activity. The Russians were monitoring the American movements; how were they to interpret them—as the preparation for an act of aggression? At this point Washington explained its actions to Moscow on the hot line, Moscow believed the explanation, and a possible military confrontation was prevented. The hot line is evidence that the leaders of the system can come to their senses a moment before it is too late and that they recognize that human dialogue is a safer way to solve dangerous confrontations than the moves dictated by the computers. But considering the whole trend, the hot line is a weak protection for the survival of mankind, since the two players might miss the right moment for explanation, or at least for its credibility.

Thus far I have only spoken of the need for certainty in the economic and political strategic processes. But the modern system satisfies this need in many other aspects. The personal career is made predictable: grades from primary school on through high school and college, plus psychological tests, permit the prediction of a person's career—subject, of course, to the economic fluctuations of the economic system. In fact, there is a great feeling of uncertainty and anxiety that besets the life of a man who wants to make his way up the ladder of the big corporation. He can fall at any point; he can fail to reach the aspired goal and become a failure in the eyes of his family and friends. But this anxiety only increases his wish for certainty. If he fails in spite of the certainty his methods of decision making offer him, he at least need not blame himself.

The same need to be certain exists in the realm of thought, feeling, and aesthetic appreciation. By the growth of literacy and of the mass media, the individual learns quickly which thoughts are "right," which behavior is correct, which feeling is normal, which taste is "in." All he has to do is to be receptive to the signals of the media, and he can be certain not to make a mistake. The fashion magazines tell what style to like and the book clubs what books to read, and to top it all, recent methods of finding proper marriage partners are based on the decisions of computers.

Our age has found a substitute for God: the impersonal calculation. This new god has turned into an idol to whom all men may be sacrificed. A new concept of the sacred and unquestionable is arising: that of calculability, probability, factuality.

We must address ourselves now to the question, What is wrong with the principle that if we give the computer all the facts, the computer can make the best possible decisions about future action?

What are facts? In themselves, even if correct and not distorted by personal or political bias, not only can facts be meaningless they can be untrue by their very selection, taking attention away from what is relevant, or scattering and fragmenting one's thinking so much that one is less capable of making meaningful decisions the more "information" one has received. The selection of facts implies evaluation and choice. The awareness of this is a necessary condition of making rational use of facts. An important statement about facts has been made by Whitehead. "The basis of all authority," he wrote in *The Function of Reason,* "is the supremacy of fact over thought. Yet this contrast of fact and thought can be conceived fallaciously. For thought is a factor in the fact of experience. Thus the immediate fact is what it is, partly by reason of the thought involved in it." [21]

Facts must be *relevant*. But relevant to what or to whom? If I am informed that A has been in prison for having wounded a rival in a state of intense jealousy, I have been informed about a fact. I can formulate the same information by saying that A was in jail, or that A was (or is) a violent man, or A was (or is) a jealous man; yet all these facts say very little about A. Maybe he is a very intense man, a proud man, a man of great integrity; maybe my factual information fails to inform me that when A speaks with children his eyes light up and he is concerned and helpful. This fact may have been omitted because it did not seem relevant to the datum of this crime; besides, it is—as yet—difficult for the computer to register a certain expression in a man's eyes, or to observe and code the fine nuances of the expression of his mouth.

To put it briefly, "facts" are interpretations of events, and the interpretation presupposes certain concerns which constitute the event's relevance. The crucial question is to be aware of what my concern is and hence of what the facts have to be in order to be relevant. Am I the man's friend, or a detective, or simply a man who wants to see the total man in his humanity? Aside from being aware of my concern, I would have to know all the details about the episode—and even then perhaps the details would not tell me how to evaluate his act. Nothing short of knowing *him,* in his individuality and suchness, his character—including the elements he himself may not be aware of—would permit me to evaluate his act; but in order to be well informed, I would also have to know myself, my own value system, what of it is genuine and what of it is ideology, my interests—selfish or otherwise. The fact, presented merely descriptively, may make me either more or less informed, and it is well

---

[21] Beacon paperback edition, 1958, p. 80.

known that there is no more effective way of distortion than to offer nothing but a series of "facts."

What holds true in this example of how to evaluate one episode in the life of a man is all the more complicated and consequential when we speak of facts pertaining to political and social life. If we show for a fact that Communists are taking steps to assume power in a Far East country, does this fact imply that they threaten to conquer all of Southeast Asia, or all of Asia? Would the latter mean that they threaten the "existence" of the United States? Does a threat to the "existence" of the United States mean a threat to the physical existence of Americans, or to our social system, or to our freedom of expression and action, or does it mean that they want to replace our elite in the area with one of their own? Which of these possible outcomes would justify or demand the possible destruction of 100 million Americans, or of all life? The "fact" of the Communist threats assumes a different meaning according to the evaluation of the total strategy and planning of the Communists. But who are the Communists? The Soviet government, the Chinese government, or who? And who is the Soviet government? That of Kosygin-Brezhnev, or of their successors who may gain power if their present strategy fails?

What I want to show is that the one fact from which we start means nothing without the evaluation of the whole system, which means an analysis of a process in which we as observers are also included. Eventually it must be stated that the very fact of having decided to select certain events as facts has an effect on ourselves. By this decision we have committed ourselves to move in a certain direction, and this commitment determines our further selection of facts. The same holds true for our opponents. They also are influenced by their own selection of facts, as well as by ours.

But not only the facts themselves are selected and ordered according to values; the programing of the computer itself is based on built-in and often unconscious values. The principle that the more we produce the better is in itself a value judgment. If instead we believed that our system should be conducive to optimum human activeness and aliveness, we would program differently and other facts would become relevant. The illusion of the certainty of the computer decision, shared by a large sector of the public and by many decision makers, rests upon the erroneous assumptions (a) that facts are objective "givens," and (b) that the programing is norm-free.[22]

All planning, whether with or without the use of computers, depends on the norms and values that underlie the planning. Planning itself is one of the most progressive steps the human race has taken. But it can be a curse if it is "blind" planning, in which man abdicates his own decision, value judgment, and responsibility. If it is alive, responsive, "open" planning, in which the human ends are in full awareness and guiding the planning process, it will be a blessing. The computer facilitates planning tremendously, but its use does not really alter the fundamental principle of the proper relationship between means and ends; only its abuse will.

---

[22] H. Ozbekhan, in a very felicitous concept, has stated that "normative" planning must precede "strategic" and "tactical" planning.

Chapter IV

What Does It Mean to Be Human?

1. HUMAN NATURE AND ITS VARIOUS MANIFESTATIONS

Having discussed the present situation of man in technological society, our next step is to examine the problem of what can be done to humanize the technological society. But before we can take this step, we must ask ourselves what it is to be human—that is, what is the human element which we have to consider as an essential factor in the functioning of the social system.

This undertaking goes beyond what is called "psychology." It should more properly be called a "science of man," a discipline which deals with the data of history, sociology, psychology, theology, mythology, physiology, economics, and art, as far as they are relevant to the understanding of man. What I can do in this chapter is necessarily most restricted. I have chosen to discuss those aspects which seem to me most necessary in the context of this book and with regard to the readers to whom it is addressed.

Man was—and still is—easily seduced into accepting a particular *form* of being human as his *essence*. To the degree to which this happens, man defines his humanity in terms of the society with which he identifies himself. However, while this has been the rule, there have been exceptions. There were always men who looked beyond the dimensions of their own society—and while they may have been called fools or criminals in their time they are the roster of great men as far as the record of human history is concerned—and visualized something which can be called universally human and which is not identical with what a particular society assumes human nature to be. There were always men who were bold and imaginative enough to see beyond the frontiers of their own social existence.

It might be helpful to recall a few definitions of "man" which may encompass in one word that which is specifically human. Man has been defined as Homo faber— the tool maker. Indeed, man is a tool maker, but our ancestors before they were fully human were tool makers too.[1]

Man has been defined as Homo sapiens, but in this definition all depends on what is meant by *sapiens*. To use thought for the purpose of finding better means for survival and ways to achieve what we want—this capacity animals also have, and there is at best a quantitative difference between man and animals as far as this kind of achievement is concerned. If, however, one means by *sapiens* knowledge in the sense of thought which tries to understand the core of phenomena, thought that penetrates from the deceptive surface to what is "really real," thought the purpose of which is not to manipulate but to comprehend, then Homo sapiens would, indeed, be a correct definition of man.

Man has been defined as Homo ludens—man the player,[2] play meaning nonpurposeful activity transcending the immediate needs for survival. Indeed from the time of the creators of the cave paintings to the present day, man has indulged in nonpurposeful activities.

---

[1] See Lewis Mumford's discussion of this point in his *The Myth of the Machine*.

[2] Cf. Johan Huizinga, *Homo Ludens: A Study of the Play Element in Culture;* also, Gustav Bally, *Vom Ursprung und von den Grenzen der Freiheit; Eine Deutung des Spiels bei Tier und Mensch (Of the Origin and of the Limitations of Freedom; and Interpretation of Play in Animal and Man),* (Basel: Schwabe, 1945).

Two other definitions of man might be added. One: Homo negans—man who can say "no," although most men say "yes" when their survival or their advantage requires it. From a statistical standpoint on human behavior, man should be called, rather, the yes-man. But from the standpoint of the human potential, man is distinguished from all other animals by his capacity to say "no," by his affirmation of truth, love, integrity, even at the expense of physical survival.

Another definition of man would be Homo esperans —the hoping man. As I have indicated in the second chapter, to hope is an essential condition of being human. If man has given up all hope, he has entered the gates of hell—whether he knows it or not—and he has left behind him his own humanity.

Perhaps the most significant definition of the species characteristic of man has been given by Marx, who defined it as "free, conscious activity." [3] Later I shall discuss the meaning of this concept.

Probably more such definitions could be added to the ones just mentioned, but they still do no justice to the question: What does it mean to be human? They emphasize only certain elements of being human without trying to give a more complete and systematic answer.

Any attempt to give an answer will immediately meet with the objection that at the very best such an answer is no more than metaphysical speculation, perhaps poetic, but at any rate the expression of subjective preference rather than a statement of any definitely ascertainable reality. These last words call to mind the theoretical physicist who might speak of his own concepts in terms of an objective reality and yet disclaim

---

[3] It is worthwhile to note that Marx criticized Aristotle's famous definition of man as a political animal and replaced it with the concept of man as a social animal and that he attacked Franklin's definition of man as a tool-making animal as "characteristic of Yankeedom."

any final statement he might make about the nature of matter. Indeed, no final statement about what it means to be human can be made now: it is possible that it may never be able to be made even if human evolution were to far transcend the present point of history, in which man has hardly begun to be fully human. But a skeptical attitude toward the possibility of making final statements about the nature of man does not mean that a number of statements cannot be made which have a scientific character, that is to say, which draw conclusions from observing the facts, conclusions which are correct in spite of the fact that the motivation to find the answer was the wish for a happier life; on the contrary, as Whitehead put it: "The function of Reason is to promote the art of life." [4]

What knowledge can we draw on in order to answer the question, what does it mean to be human? The answer cannot lie in the direction which such answers have often taken: that man is good or bad, loving or destructive, gullible or independent, etc. Obviously, man can be all this just as he can be musical or tone-deaf, sensitive to painting or color-blind, a saint or a rascal. All these and many other qualities are various *possibilities* of being human. In fact, they are all within each one of us. To be fully aware of one's humanity means to be aware that, as Terence said, *"Homo sum, nil humani a me alienum puto"* (I am a man and nothing human is alien to me); that each one carries all of humanity within himself—the saint as well as the criminal; as Goethe put it, that there is no crime of which one cannot imagine oneself to be the author. All these *manifestations of humanity* are not the answer to what does it mean to be human. They are only answering the question, *how different can we be and yet be human?* If we want to know what it means to be human, we must be prepared to find answers not in terms of different human possibilities, but in terms of the very conditions of human exist-

---

[4] *The Function of Reason* (Boston: Beacon Press, 1958), p. 4.

ence from which all these possibilities spring as possible alternatives. These conditions can be recognized as a result not of metaphysical speculation but of the examination of the data of anthropology, history, child psychology, individual and social psychopathology.

2. THE CONDITIONS OF HUMAN EXISTENCE

What are these conditions? There are essentially two, which are interrelated. First, the decrease of instinctual determinism the higher we go in animal evolution, reaching its lowest point in man, in whom the force of instinctual determinism moves toward the zero end of the scale.

Second, the tremendous increase in size and complexity of the brain in comparison with body weight, in the second half of the Pleistocene. This enlarged neocortex is the basis for awareness, imagination, and all those facilities such as speech and symbol-making which characterize human existence.

Man, lacking the instinctual equipment of the animal, is not as well equipped for flight or for attack as animals are. He does not "know" infallibly, as the salmon knows where to return to the river in order to spawn its young and as many birds know where to go south in the winter and where to return in the summer. His decisions are *not made for him* by instinct. *He* has to make *them*. He is faced with alternatives and there is a risk of failure in every decision he makes. The price that man pays for consciousness is insecurity. He can stand his insecurity by being aware and accepting the human condition, and by the hope that he will not fail even though he has no guarantee of success. He has no certainty; the only certain prediction he can make is: "I shall die."

Man is born as a freak of nature, being within nature

and yet transcending it. He has to find principles of action and decision-making which replace the principles of instinct. He has to have a frame of orientation which permits him to organize a consistent picture of the world as a condition for consistent actions. He has to fight not only against the dangers of dying, starving, and being hurt, but also against another danger which is specifically human: that of becoming insane. In other words, he has to protect himself not only against the danger of losing his life but also against the danger of losing his mind. The human being, born under the conditions described here, would indeed go mad if he did not find a frame of reference which permitted him to feel at home in the world in some form and to escape the experience of utter helplessness, disorientation, and uprootedness. There are many ways in which man can find a solution to the task of staying alive and of remaining sane. Some are better than others and some are worse. By "better" is meant a way conducive to greater strength, clarity, joy, independence; and by "worse" the very opposite. But more important than finding the *better* solution is finding some solution which is viable.

The foregoing thoughts raise the problem of man's malleability. Some anthropologists and other observers of man have believed that man is infinitely malleable. At first glance, this seems to be so. Just as he can eat meat or vegetables or both, he can live as a slave and as a free man, in scarcity or abundance, in a society which values love and one which values destruction. Indeed, man can do almost anything, or, perhaps better, the social order can do almost anything to man. The "almost" is important. Even if the social order can do everything to man —starve him, torture him, imprison him, or overfeed him—this cannot be done without certain consequences which follow from the very conditions of human existence. Man, if utterly deprived of all stimuli and pleasure, will be incapable of performing work, certainly any skilled work.[5] If he is not that utterly destitute, he will tend to rebel if you make him a slave; he will tend to be violent if life is too boring; he will tend to lose all creativity if you make him into a machine. Man in this respect is not different from animals or from inanimate matter. You may get certain animals into the zoo, but they will not reproduce, and others will become violent although they are not violent in freedom.[6] You can heat water above a certain temperature and it will become steam; or cool it below a certain temperature and it will become solid. But you cannot make steam by lowering its temperature. The history of man shows precisely what you can do to man and at the same time what you *cannot* do. If man were infinitely malleable, there would have been no revolutions; there would have been no change because a culture would have succeeded in making man submit to its patterns without his resistance. But man, being only *relatively* malleable, has always reacted with protest against conditions which made the disequilibrium between the social order and his human needs too drastic or unbearable. The attempt to reduce this disequilibrium and the need to establish a more acceptable and desirable solution is at the very core of the dynamism of the evolution of man in history. Man's protest arose not only because of material suffering; specifically human needs, to be discussed later, are an equally strong motivation for revolution and the dynamics of change.

---

[5] The recent experiments with sensory deprivation show that extreme forms of the absence of stimuli to which man can respond are able to produce symptoms of severe mental illness.

[6] A similar fact has been discovered in psychotic patients who live on farms or in nonprisonlike conditions. They showed little violence under these conditions of noncoercion; this proved that the alleged reason for their previous prisonlike treatment, that is, their violence, produced the very result which the treatment was supposed to reduce or to control.

3. THE NEED FOR FRAMES OF ORIENTATION AND DEVOTION

There are various possible answers to the question that human existence raises. They are centered around two problems: one, the need for a frame of orientation, and the other the need for a frame of devotion.

What are the answers to the need for a frame of orientation? The one overriding answer which man has found so far is one which can also be observed among animals —to submit to a strong leader who is supposed to know what is best for the group, who plans and orders and who promises to everyone that by following him he acts in the best interests of all. In order to enforce allegiance to the leader, or, to put it differently, to give the individual enough faith to believe in the leader, the leader is assumed to have qualities transcending those of any of his subjects. He is supposed to be omnipotent, omniscient, sacred; he is a god himself or a god's viceroy or a high priest, knowing the secrets of the cosmos and performing the rituals necessary for its continuity. To be sure, the leaders have usually used promises and threats to manipulate submission. But this is by no means the whole story. Man, as long as he has not arrived at a higher form of his own evolution, has needed the leader and was only too eager to believe the fantastic stories proving the legitimacy of the king, god, father, monarch, priest, etc. This need for the leader still exists in the most enlightened societies of our day. Even in countries like the United States or the Soviet Union, decisions affecting the life and death of everyone are left to a small group of leaders or to one man who is acting under the formal mandate of the constitution—whether it is called "democratic" or "socialist." In their wish for security, men love their own dependence, especially if it is made easy for them by the relative comfort of material life and by ideologies which call brainwashing "education" and submission "freedom."

There is no need to seek for the roots of this submissiveness in the phenomenon of dominance-submission among animals. In fact, in quite a few animals it is not as extreme or widespread as it is in man, and the very conditions of human existence would require submission even if we disregarded our animal past completely. However, there is one decisive difference. *Man is not bound to be sheep.* In fact, inasmuch as he is not an animal, man has an interest in being related to and conscious of reality, to touch the earth with his feet, as in the Greek legend of Antaeus; man is stronger the more fully he is in touch with reality. As long as he is only sheep and his reality is essentially nothing but the fiction built up by his society for more convenient manipulation of men and things, he is weak as a man. Any change in the social pattern threatens him with intense insecurity and even madness because his whole relationship with reality is mediated by the fictitious reality which is presented to him as real. The more he can grasp reality on his own and not only as a datum with which society provides him, the more secure he feels because the less completely dependent he is on consensus and hence the less threatened by social change. Man qua man has an inherent tendency to enlarge his knowledge of reality and that means to approximate the truth. We are not dealing here with a metaphysical concept of truth but with a concept of increasing approximation, which means decreasing fiction and delusion. In comparison with the importance of this increase or decrease of one's grasp of reality, the question whether there is a final truth about anything remains entirely abstract and irrelevant. The process of increasing awareness is nothing but the process of awakening, of opening one's eyes and seeing what is in front of one. Awareness means doing away with illusions and, to the degree that this is accomplished, it is a process of liberation.

In spite of the fact that there is a tragic disproportion

between intellect and emotion at the present moment in industrial society, there is no denying the fact that the history of man is a history of growing awareness. This awareness refers to the facts of nature outside of himself as well as to his own nature. While man still wears blinders, in many respects his critical reason has discovered a great deal about the nature of the universe and the nature of man. He is still very much at the beginning of this process of discovery, and the crucial question is whether the destructive power which his present knowledge has given him will permit him to go on extending this knowledge to an extent which is unimaginable today, or whether he will destroy himself before he can build an ever-fuller picture of reality on the present foundations.

If this development is to take place, one condition is necessary: that the social contradictions and irrationalities which throughout most of man's history have forced upon him a "false consciousness"—in order to justify domination and submission respectively—disappear or at least are reduced to such a degree that the apology for the existent social order does not paralyze man's capacity for critical thought. Of course, this is not a matter of what is first and what is second. Awareness of existing reality and of alternatives for its improvement helps to change reality, and every improvement in reality helps the clarification of thought. Today, when scientific reasoning has reached a peak, the transformation of society, burdened by the inertia of previous circumstances, into a sane society could permit the average man to use his reason with the same objectivity to which we are accustomed from the scientists. This is a matter not primarily of superior intelligence but of the disappearance of irrationality from social life—an irrationality which necessarily leads to confusion of the mind.

Man not only has a mind and is in need of a frame of orientation which permits him to make some sense of and to structuralize the world around him; he has also a heart and a body which need to be tied emotionally to the world—to man and to nature. As I mentioned before, the animal's ties to the world are given, mediated by his instincts. Man, set apart by his self-awareness and the capacity to feel lonely, would be a helpless bit of dust driven by the winds if he did not find emotional ties which satisfied his need to be related and unified with the world beyond his own person. But in contrast to the animal, he has several alternative ways thus to be tied. As in the case of his mind, some possibilities are better than others; but what he needs most in order to retain his sanity is some tie to which he feels securely related. The one who has no such tie is, by definition, insane, incapable of any emotional connection with his fellow man.

The easiest and most frequent form of man's relatedness is his "primary ties" to where he comes from—to blood, soil, clan, to mother and father, or, in a more complex society, to his nation, religion, or class. These ties are not primarily of a sexual nature, but they fulfill the longing of a man who has not grown up to become himself, to overcome the sense of unbearable separateness. This solution of the problem of human separateness by continuing what I have called the "primary ties" —which are natural and necessary for the infant in his relationship to his mother—is obvious when we study the primitive cults of the worship of the soil, of lakes, of mountains, or of animals, often accompanied by the individual's symbolic identification with these animals (totem animals). We see it in the matriarchal religions in which the Great Mother and goddesses of fertility and of the soil are worshiped.[7] There seems to be an attempt to overcome these primary ties to mother and earth in the patriarchal religions, in which the great father, the god, king, tribal chief, law, or state are objects of worship. But although this step from the matriarchal to the patriarchal cult in society is a progressive one, the two forms have in common the fact that man finds his emo-

---

[7] Cf. Bachofen's and Briffault's work on matriarchal societies.

tional ties to a superior authority, which he blindly obeys. By remaining bound to nature, to mother or father, man indeed succeeds in feeling at home in the world, but he pays a tremendous price for this security, that of submission, dependence, and a blockage to the full development of his reason and of his capacity to love. He remains a child when he should become an adult.[8]

The primitive forms of incestuous ties to mother, soil, race, etc., of benign and of malignant ecstasies can disappear only if man finds a higher form of feeling at home in the world, if not only his intellect develops, but also his capacity to feel related without submitting, at home without being imprisoned, intimate without being stifled. On a social scale, this new vision was expressed from the middle of the second millennium B.C. to the middle of the first millennium—one of the most remarkable periods in human history. The solution to human existence was no longer sought in the return to nature nor in blind obedience to the father figure, but in a new vision that man can again feel at home in the world and overcome his sense of frightening loneliness; that he can achieve this by the full development of his human powers, of his capacity to love, to use his reason, to create and enjoy beauty, to share his humanity with all his

---

[8] Today the many individual cases of "mother fixation" are explained by orthodox psychoanalysts as a result of an undissolved sexual tie to mother. This explanation ignores the fact that this tie to mother is only one of the possible answers to the predicament of human existence. The dependent individual of the twentieth century, living in a culture which in its social aspects expects him to be independent, is confused and often neurotic because his society does not provide him—as do more primitive societies—with the social and religious patterns to satisfy his need for dependency. The fixation to mother is a personal expression of one of the answers to human existence which some cultures have expressed in religious forms. It is an answer, though one which conflicts with the full development of the individual.

fellow men. Buddhism, Judaism, and Christianity proclaimed this new vision.

The new bond which permits man to feel at one with all men is fundamentally different from that of the submission-bond to father and mother; it is the harmonious bond of brotherhood in which solidarity and human ties are not vitiated by restriction of freedom, either emotionally or intellectually. This is the reason why the solution of brotherliness is not one of subjective preference. It is the only one which satisfies the two needs of man: to be closely related and at the same time to be free, to be part of a whole and to be independent. It is a solution which has been experienced by many individuals and also by groups, religious or secular, which were and are able to develop the bonds of solidarity together with unrestricted individuality and independence.

4. SURVIVAL AND TRANS-SURVIVAL NEEDS

In order to understand fully the human predicament and the possible choices man is confronted with, I must discuss another type of fundamental conflict inherent in human existence. Inasmuch as man has a body and bodily needs essentially the same as those of the animal, he has a built-in striving for physical survival, even though the methods he uses do not have the instinctive, reflexlike character which are more developed in the animal. Man's body makes him want to survive regardless of circumstances, even of happiness or unhappiness, slavery or freedom. As a consequence, man must work or force others to work for him. In the past history of man, most of man's time was spent on food gathering. I use the term "food gathering" here in a very broad sense. With the animal, it essentially means gathering the food in the quantity and quality his instinctive apparatus suggest to him. In man there is much greater flexibility in the kind of food he can choose; but more than this, man, once he begins the process of civilization, works not only to gather food but to make clothes, to build shelters, and, in the more advanced cultures, to produce the many things which are not strictly necessary for his physical survival but which have developed as real needs forming the material basis for a life which permits the development of culture.

If man were satisfied to spend his life by making a living, there would be no problem. Although he does not have the instinct of ants, an antlike existence would nevertheless be perfectly tolerable. However, it is part of the human condition that man is not satisfied with being an ant, that aside from this sphere of biological or material survival, there is a sphere characteristic of man which one can call the trans-survival or trans-utilitarian sphere.

What does this mean? Precisely because man has awareness and imagination, and because he has the potential of freedom, he has an inherent tendency not to be, as Einstein once put it, "dice thrown out of the cup." He wants not only to know what is necessary in order to survive, but he wants to understand what human life is about. He is the only case of life being aware of itself. He wants to make use of those faculties which he has developed in the process of history and which serve more than the process of mere biological survival. Hunger and sex, as purely physiological phenomena, belong to the sphere of survival. (Freud's psychological system suffers from the main error which was part of the mechanistic materialism of his time and which led him to build a psychology on those drives which serve survival.) But man has passions which are specifically human and transcend the function of survival.

Nobody has expressed this more clearly than Marx: "Passion is man's faculties striving to obtain their object." [9] In this statement, passion is considered as a concept of relation or relatedness. The dynamism of human nature inasmuch as it is human is primarily rooted in this need of man *to express his faculties in relation to the world rather than in his need to use the world as a means for the satisfaction of his physiological necessities*. This means: because I have eyes, I have the need to see; because I have ears, I have the need to hear; because I have a mind, I have the need to think; and because I have a heart, I have the need to feel. In short, because I am a man, I am in need of man and of the world. Marx makes very clear what he means by "human faculties" which relate to the world in a passionate way: "His *human* relationships to the world—seeing, hearing, smelling, tasting, touching, thinking, observing, feeling, desiring, acting, loving—in which all the organs of his individuality are the . . . active expression (*Betaetigung*) of human reality . . . In practice I can only relate myself in a human way to a thing when the thing is related in a human way to man." [10]

Man's drives, inasmuch as they are trans-utilitarian, are an expression of a fundamental and specifically human need: the need to be related to man and nature and to confirm himself in this relatedness.

These two forms of human existence, that of food gathering for the purpose of survival in a narrow or broader sense and that of free and spontaneous activity expressing man's faculties and seeking for meaning beyond utilitarian work, are inherent in man's existence. Each society and each man has its own particular rhythm in which these two forms of living make their appearance. What matters is the relative strength which each of the two have and which one dominates the other.

---

[9] In "Economic and Philosophical Manuscripts," English translation by T. Bottomore in E. Fromm, *Marx's Concept of Man* (New York: Ungar, 1961).

[10] *Ibid.*, p. 132.

Both action and thought share in the double nature of this polarity. Activity on the level of survival is what one usually calls work. Activeness on the trans-survival level is what one calls play, or all those activities related to cult, ritual, and art. Thought also appears in two forms, one serving the function of survival and one serving the function of knowledge in the sense of understanding and intuiting. This distinction of survival and trans-survival thought is very important for the understanding of consciousness and the so-called unconscious. Our conscious thought is that type of thinking, linked with language, which follows the social categories of thought imprinted in our thinking from early childhood.[11] Our consciousness is essentially the awareness of such phenomena which the social filter composed of language, logic, and taboos permits us to become aware of. Those phenomena which cannot pass the social filter remain unconscious or, more accurately speaking, we are unaware of everything that cannot penetrate to our consciousness because the social filter blocks its entry. This is the reason why consciousness is determined by the structure of society. However, this statement is only descriptive. Inasmuch as man has to work within a given society, his need for survival tends to make him accept the social conceptualizations and hence to repress that which he would be aware of had his consciousness been imprinted with different schemata. This is not the place to give examples of this hypothesis, but it is not difficult for the reader to find his own example if he studies other cultures. The categories of thought in the industrial age are that of quantification, abstraction and comparison, of profit and loss, of efficiency and inefficiency. The member of a consumer society of the present day, for exam-

---

[11] The work of Benjamin Whorf has shown the intimate connection between language and differences in the modes of thought and experience. Cf. the important contribution to this problem by Ernest G. Schachtel in *Metamorphosis, op. cit.*, and in previous papers.

ple, does not need to repress sexual desires because sex is not tabooed by the schemata of industrial society. The member of the middle class of the nineteenth century who was busy accumulating capital and investing it rather than consuming it, had to repress sexual desires because they did not fit into the acquisitive and hoarding mood of his society, or, more correctly, of the middle classes. If we think of medieval or Greek society or of such cultures as the Pueblo Indians' we can easily recognize that they were very conscious of different aspects of life to which their social filter granted entry into consciousness while others were tabooed.

The most eminent case in which man does not have to accept the social categories of his society is when he is asleep. Sleep is that state of being in which man is free from the need to take care of his survival. While he is awake, he is largely determined by the survival function; while he is asleep, he is a free man. As a result, his thinking is not subject to the thought categories of his society and shows that peculiar creativity which we find in dreams. In dreams, man creates symbols and has insights into the nature of life and of his own personality which he is incapable of having while he is the creature busy with food gathering and defense. Often, indeed, this lack of contact with social reality can cause him to have experiences and thoughts which are archaic, primitive, malignant, but even those are authentic and represent *him* rather than the thought patterns of his society. In dreams, the individual transcends the narrow boundaries of his society and becomes fully human. That is why Freud's discovery of dream interpretation, even though he looked basically for the repressed sexual instinct, has paved the way for the understanding of the uncensored humanity which is in all of us. (Sometimes children, before they have been sufficiently indoctrinated by the process of education, and psychotics who have severed all relationships to the social world manifest insights and creative artistic possibilities which the adapted adult cannot recover.)

But dreams are only a special case of that trans-survival life of man. Its main expression is in rituals, symbols, painting, poetry, drama, and music. Our utilitarian thinking has, quite logically, tried to interpret all these phenomena as serving the survival function (a vulgarized Marxism has sometimes allied itself in substance although not in form with this type of materialism). More profound observers like Lewis Mumford and others have emphasized the fact that the cave paintings in France and the ornaments on primitive pottery, as well as more advanced forms of art, have no utilitarian purpose. One might say that their function is to help the survival of man's spirit, but not that of man's body.

Here lies the connection between *beauty* and *truth*. Beauty is not the opposite of the *"ugly,"* but of the *"false"*; it is the sensory statement of the suchness of a thing or a person. To create beauty presupposes, in terms of Zen Buddhist thinking, the state of mind in which one has emptied oneself in order to fill oneself with what one portrays so that one becomes it. "Beautiful" and "ugly" are merely conventional categories which vary from culture to culture. A good example of our failure to comprehend beauty is the average person's tendency to cite a "sunset" as an example of the beautiful, as if rain or fog were not just as beautiful, although sometimes less pleasant for the body.

All great art is by its very essence in conflict with the society with which it coexists. It expresses the truth about existence regardless of whether this truth serves or hinders the survival purposes of a given society. All great art is revolutionary because it touches upon the reality of man and questions the reality of the various transitory forms of human society. Even an artist who is a political reactionary is more revolutionary—if he is a great artist—than the artists of "socialist realism" who only mirror the particular form of their society with its contradictions.

It is an astonishing fact that art has not been forbidden throughout history by the powers that were and are. There are perhaps several reasons for this. One is that without art man is starved and perhaps not even useful for the practical purposes of his society. Another is that by his particular form and perfection the great artist was an "outsider" and hence while he stimulated and gave life he was not dangerous because he did not translate his art into political terms. Besides that, art usually reached only the educated or politically less dangerous classes of society. The artists have been the court jesters of all past history. They were permitted to say the truth because they presented it in its particular but socially restricted artistic form.

The industrial society of our time prides itself on the fact that millions of people have a chance and, in fact, use the chance to listen to excellent live or recorded music, to see art in the many museums in the country, and to read the masterworks of human literature from Plato to Russell in easily available, inexpensive editions. No doubt for a small minority this encounter with art and literature is a genuine experience. For the vast majority, "culture" is another article of consumption and a status symbol inasmuch as having seen the "right" pictures, knowing the "right" music, and having read the good books indicates college education and hence is useful for climbing the social ladder. The best of art has been transformed into an article of consumption, and that is to say it is reacted to in an alienated fashion. The proof of this is that many of the very same people who go to concerts, listen to classical music, and buy a paperback Plato view tasteless and vulgar offerings on television without disgust. If their experience with art were genuine, they would turn off their television sets when they are offered artless, banal "drama."

Yet man's longing for that which is dramatic, that which touches upon the fundamentals of human experience, is not dead. While most of the drama offered in theaters or on the screen is either a nonartistic commodity or is consumed in an alienated fashion, the modern "drama" is primitive and barbaric when it is genuine.

In our day the longing for drama is manifested most genuinely in the attraction which real or fictionalized accidents, crimes, and violence have for most people. An automobile accident or fire will attract crowds of people who watch with great intensity. Why do they do so? Simply because the elemental confrontation with life and death breaks into the surface of conventional experience and fascinates people hungry for drama. For the same reason, nothing sells a newspaper better than reports of crime and violence. The fact is that while on the surface the Greek drama or Rembrandt's paintings are held in the highest esteem, their real substitutes are crime, murder, and violence, either directly visible on the television screen or reported in the newspapers.

5. "HUMANE EXPERIENCES"

Contemporary industrial man has undergone an intellectual development to which we do not yet see any limits. Simultaneously he tends to emphasize those sensations and feeling experiences which he shares with the animal: sexual desires, aggression, fright, hunger, and thirst. The decisive question is, Are there any emotional experiences which are specifically human and which do not correspond to what we know as being rooted in the lower brain? The view is often voiced that the tremendous development of the neocortex has made it possible for man to arrive at an ever-increasing intellectual capacity but that his lower brain is hardly different from that of his primate ancestors and hence that, emotionally speaking, he has not developed and can at best deal with his "drives" only by repression or control.[12]

I submit that there are specifically human experiences which are neither of an intellectual character nor identical with those feeling experiences which by and large are similar to those of the animal. Not being competent in the field of neurophysiology, I can only guess [13] that particular relations between the large neocortex and the old brain are the basis for these specifically· human feelings. There are reasons to speculate that the specifically human affective experiences like love, tenderness, compassion, and all affects which do not serve the function of survival are based on the interaction between the new and the old brain; hence, that man is not distinguished from the animal only by his intellect, but by new affective qualities which result from the interaction between the neocortex and the base of animal emotionality. The student of human nature can observe these specifically human affects empirically and he cannot be deterred by the fact that neurophysiology has not yet demonstrated the neurophysiological basis for this sector of experiences. As with many other fundamental problems of human nature, the student of the science of man cannot be placed in the position of neglecting his observations because neurophysiology has not yet given the green light. Each science, neurophysiology as well as psychology, has its own method and necessarily will deal with such problems as it can handle at a given point in its scientific development. It is the task of the psychologist to challenge the neurophysiologist, urging him to confirm or deny his findings, just as it is his task to be aware of neurophysiological conclu-

---

[12] This view, for instance, is held by as profound a biologist as Ludwig von Bertalanfy, who, starting from another discipline, arrives in many other aspects at conclusions similar to the ones expressed in this book.

[13] I gratefully acknowledge the stimulating personal communications by the late Dr. Rául Hernandez Péon, Mexico, and Dr. Manfred Clynes, Rockland State Hospital, New York.

sions and to be stimulated and challenged by them. Both sciences, psychology and neurophysiology, are young and very much at their inception. They must develop relatively independently and yet remain in close touch with each other, mutually challenging and stimulating.[14]

In the discussion of the specifically human experiences, which I shall call "humane experiences" in what follows, we might best begin with the examination of "greed." Greed is a common quality of desires by which men are *driven* to achieve a certain goal. In the non-greedy feeling, man is not driven, he is not passive, but he is free and active.

Greed can be motivated in two ways: (1) By a physiological imbalance which produces the greedy desire for food, drink, etc. Once the physiological need is satisfied, the greed ceases, unless the imbalance is chronic. (2) By a psychological imbalance, especially the presence of increased anxiety, loneliness, insecurity, lack of identity, etc., which is alleviated by the satisfaction of certain desires like those for food, sexual satisfaction, power, fame, property, etc. This type of greed is, in principle, insatiable, unless a person's anxiety, etc., ceases or is greatly reduced. The first type of greed is reactive to circumstances; the second is inherent in the character structure.

The greedy feeling is highly egocentric. Whether it is hunger, thirst, or sexual desire, the greedy person wants something for himself exclusively, and that by which he

---

[14] It may be noted in passing that as far as the "drives" which function for the sake of survival are concerned, it does not sound implausible that a computer could be developed which would parallel this whole aspect of feeling sensations, but as far as the specifically human feeling aspect, which does not serve survival purposes, is concerned it seems difficult to imagine that a computer could be constructed which would parallel nonsurvival functions. One might even say that the "humane experience" could be negatively defined as one which cannot be duplicated by a machine.

satisfies his desire is only a means for his own purposes. This is obvious when we speak of hunger and thirst, but it is also the case when we speak of sexual arousal in its greedy form where the other person becomes primarily an *object*. In the nongreedy feeling, there is little ego-centricity. The experience is not needed to preserve one's life, to allay anxiety, or to satisfy or enhance one's ego; it does not serve to still a powerful tension, but begins precisely where necessity in the sense of survival or stilling of anxiety ends. In the nongreedy feeling, the person can let go of himself, is not compulsively holding on to what he has and what he wants to have, but is open and responsive.

Sexual experience can be simply sensuously pleasurable without the depth of love but also without a marked degree of greed. The sexual arousal is physiologically stimulated, and it may or may not lead to human intimacy. The opposite of this kind of sexual desire is characterized by an opposite sequence, namely, that love creates sexual desire. This means, more concretely speaking, that a man and a woman may feel a deep sense of love for each other in terms of concern, knowledge, intimacy, and responsibility, and that this deep human experience arouses the wish for physical union. It is obvious that this second type of sexual desire will occur more frequently, although by no means exclusively so, among people beyond their mid-twenties and that it is the basis for the continuation of sexual desire in monogamous human relationships of long duration. Where this type of sexual arousal does not take place, it is natural that—aside from sexual perversions which might bind two people together for a lifetime because of the individual nature of their perversion—the merely physiological arousal will tend to require change and new sexual experiences. Both these kinds of sexual arousal are fundamentally different from the greedy one that is essentially motivated by anxiety or narcissism.

In spite of the complexity of the distinction between greedy and "free" sexuality, the distinction exists. It could be demonstrated in a volume which would be as detailed in the description of sexual relationships as Kinsey's and Masters' but which would transcend the narrowness of their points of observation. But I do not believe we have to wait for this volume to be written. Everyone who becomes aware of and sensitive to the difference can observe in himself and herself the various types of arousal, and those with more sexual experimentation than was the case in the middle class of the Victorian age may be supposed to have rich material for such observation. I say they may be *supposed* to have, because, unfortunately, increased sexual experimentation has not been combined sufficiently with greater discernment of the qualitative differences in sexual experience —although I am sure that a considerable number of people exist who, when they reflect upon these matters, can verify the validity of the distinction.

We can now proceed to discuss some other "humane experiences" without claiming that the following description is in any way exhaustive. Related to nongreedy sexual desire but different from it is *tenderness*. Freud, whose whole psychology deals exclusively with "drives," necessarily had to explain tenderness as an outcome of the sexual drive, as a goal-inhibited sexual desire. His theory made this definition necessary, but observation tends to show that tenderness is not a phenomenon which can be explained as goal-inhibited sexual desire. It is an experience *sui generis*. Its first characteristic is that it is free from greed. In the experience of tenderness, one does not want anything from the other person, not even reciprocity. It has no particular aim and purpose, not even that which is present in the relatively ungreedy form of sexuality, namely, of the final physical culmination. It is not restricted to any sex or any age. It is least of all expressible in words, except perhaps in a poem. It is most exquisitely expressed in the way in which a person may touch another, look at him or her, or in the tone of voice. One can say that it has roots in the tenderness which a mother feels toward her child, but even if this is so, human tenderness far transcends the mother's tenderness to the child because it is free from the biological tie to the child and from the narcissistic element in motherly love. It is free not only from greed but from hurry and purpose. Among all the feelings which man has created in himself during his history, there is perhaps none which surpasses tenderness in the pure quality of simply being human.

Compassion and *empathy* are two other feelings clearly related to tenderness but not entirely identical with it. The essence of compassion is that one "suffers with" or, in a broader sense, "feels with" another person. This means that one does not look at the person from the outside—the person being the "object" (never forget that "object" and "objection" have the same root) of my interest or concern—but that one puts himself into the other person. This means I experience within myself what he experiences. This is a relatedness which is not from the "I" to the "thou" but one which is characterized by the phrase: I *am* thou (*Tat Twam Asi*). Compassion or empathy implies that I experience in myself that which is experienced by the other person and hence that in this experience he and I are one. All knowledge of another person is real knowledge only if it is based on my experiencing in myself that which he experiences. If this is not the case and the person remains an object, I may know a lot *about* him but I do not *know him*.[15] Goethe has expressed this kind of knowledge very succinctly: "Man knows himself only within

---

[15] In psychoanalysis or similar forms of depth psychotherapy, a knowledge of the patient rests upon the capacity of the analyst to know *him* and not of his ability to gather enough data to know much *about* him. The data of the development and experiences of the patient are often helpful for knowing him, but they are nothing but adjuncts to that knowledge which requires no "data," but rather, complete openness to the other and openness within oneself. It might occur in the first second after seeing a person, it might occur a long time later, but the act of this knowledge is a sudden, intuitive one and not the final result of ever-increasing information about the life history of the person.

himself, and he is aware of himself within the world. Each new object truly recognized opens up a new organ within ourselves."

The possibility of this kind of knowledge based on overcoming the split between the observing subject and the observed object requires, of course, the humanistic promise which I mentioned above, namely, that every person carries within himself all of humanity; that within ourselves we are saints and criminals, although in varying degrees, and hence that there is nothing in another person which we cannot feel as part of ourselves. This experience requires that we free ourselves from the narrowness of being related only to those familiar to us, either by the fact that they are blood relations or, in a larger sense, that we eat the same food, speak the same language, and have the same "common sense." *Knowing* men in the sense of compassionate and empathetic knowledge requires that we get rid of the narrowing ties of a given society, race, or culture and penetrate to the depth of that human reality in which we are all nothing but human. True compassion and knowledge of man has been largely underrated as a revolutionary factor in the development of man, just as art has been.

Tenderness, love, and compassion are exquisite feeling experiences and generally recognized as such. I wish now to discuss some "humane experiences" which are not as clearly identified as feelings but are more frequently called attitudes. Their main difference from the experiences discussed so far lies in the fact that they do not express the same direct relatedness to another person, but are, rather, experiences which are within oneself and which only secondarily refer to other persons.

The first one among this second group I wish to describe is *"interest."* The word "interest" today has lost most of its meaning. To say "I am interested" in this or that is almost equivalent to saying "I have no particularly strong feeling about it but I am not entirely indifferent." It is one of those cover words which mask the absence of intensity and which are vague enough to cover almost anything from having an interest in a certain industrial stock to an interest in a girl. But this deterioration of meaning which is so general cannot deter us from using words in their original and deeper meaning, and that means to restore them to their own dignity. "Interest" comes from the Latin *inter-esse,* that is, "to be in-between." If I am interested, I must transcend my ego, be open to the world, and jump into it. Interest is based on activeness. It is the relatively constant attitude which permits one at any moment to grasp intellectually as well as emotionally and sensuously the world outside. The interested person becomes interesting to others because interest has an infectious quality which awakens interest in those who cannot initiate it without help. The meaning of interest becomes still clearer when we think of its opposite: curiosity. The curious person is basically passive. He wants to be fed with knowledge and sensations and can never have enough, since quantity of information is a substitute for the depth quality of knowledge. The most important realm in which curiosity is satisfied is gossip, be it the small-town gossip of the woman who sits at the window and watches with her spyglasses what is going on around her or the somewhat more elaborate gossip which fills the newspaper columns, occurs in the faculty meetings of professors as well as in the management meetings of the bureaucracy, and at the cocktail parties of the writers and artists. Curiosity, by its very nature, is insatiable, since aside from its maliciousness, it never really answers the question, Who is the other person?

Interest has many objects: persons, plants, animals, ideas, social structures, and it depends to some extent on the temperament and the specific character of a person as to what his interests are. Nevertheless the objects are secondary. Interest is an all-pervading attitude and form of relatedness to the world, and one might define it in a very broad sense as the interest of the living person in all that is alive and grows. Even when this sphere of interest in one person seems to be small, if the interest is genuine, there will be no difficulty in arousing his interest in other fields, simply because he is an interested person.

Another of the "humane experiences" to be discussed here is that of *responsibility*. Again, the word "responsibility" has lost its original meaning and is usually used as a synonym for duty. Duty is a concept in the realm of unfreedom, while responsibility is a concept in the realm of freedom.

This difference between duty and responsibility corresponds to the distinction between the authoritarian and humanistic conscience. The authoritarian conscience is essentially the readiness to follow the orders of the authorities to which one submits; it is glorified obedience. The humanistic conscience is the readiness to listen to the voice of one's own humanity and is independent of orders given by anyone else.[16]

Two other types of "humane experience" are difficult to classify in terms of feelings, affects, attitudes. But it matters little how we classify them, since all these classifications themselves are based on traditional distinctions, the validity of which is questionable. I am referring to the sense of *identity* and *integrity*.

In recent years, the problem of identity has been much in the foreground of psychological discussion, especially stimulated by the excellent work of Erik Erikson. He has spoken of the "identity crisis" and, undoubtedly, he has touched upon one of the major psychological problems of industrial society. But in my opinion, he has not gone as far or penetrated as deeply as is necessary for the full understanding of the phe-

---

[16] Freud's concept of superego is a psychological formulation of the authoritarian conscience. It implies listening to the commands and prohibitions of one's father, continued later by social authorities.

nomena of identity and identity crisis. In industrial society men are transformed into things, and things have no identity. Or do they? Is not every Ford car of a certain year and a certain model identical with every other Ford car of the same model and different from other models and vintages? Has not any dollar bill its identity; like any other dollar bill inasmuch as it has the same design, value, exchangeability, but different from any other dollar bill in terms of the differences in the quality of the paper brought about by the length of use? *Things* can be the same or different. However, if we speak of identity, we speak of a quality which does not pertain to things, but only to man.

What then is identity in a *human* sense? Among the many approaches to this question, I want to stress only the concept that identity is the experience which permits a person to say legitimately "I"—"I" as an organizing active center of the structure of all my actual or potential activities. This experience of "I" exists only in the state of spontaneous activity, but it does not exist in the state of passiveness and half-awakeness, a state in which people are sufficiently awake to go about their business but not awake enough to sense an "I" as the active center within themselves.[17] This concept of "I" is different from the concept of ego. (I do not use this term in the Freudian sense but in the popular sense of a person who, for example, has a "big ego.") The experience of my "ego" is the experience of myself as a thing, of the body I have, the memory I have—the money, the house, the social position, the power, the children, the problems I *have*. I look at myself as a thing and my social role is another attribute of thingness. Many people easily confuse the identity of ego with the identity of "I" or self. The difference is fundamental and unmistakable. The experience of ego, and

---

[17] In Eastern thought, this "I" center was sometimes felt to be located in the point between the eyes, the point where in mythological language the "third eye" used to be.

of ego-identity, is based on the concept of having. I *have* "me" as I have all other things which this "me" owns. Identity of "I" or self refers to the category of being and not of having. I am "I" only to the extent to which I am alive, interested, related, active, and to which I have achieved an integration between my appearance—to others and/or to myself—and the core of my personality. The identity crisis of our time is based essentially on the increasing alienation and reification of man, and it can be solved only to the extent to which man comes to life again, becomes active again. There are no psychological shortcuts to the solution to the identity crisis except the fundamental transformation of alienated man into living man.[18]

The increasing emphasis on ego versus self, on having versus being, finds a glaring expression in the development of our language. It has become customary for people to say, "I have insomnia," instead of saying, "I cannot sleep"; or, "I have a problem," instead of, "I feel sad, confused" or whatever it may be; or, "I have a happy marriage" (sometimes successful marriage), instead of saying, "My wife and I love each other." All categories of the process of being are transformed into categories of having. The ego, static and unmoved, relates to the world in terms of having objects, while the self is related to the world in the process of participation. Modern man *has* everything: a car, a house, a job, "kids," a marriage, problems, troubles, satisfactions— and if all that is not enough, he has his psychoanalyst. He *is* nothing.

A concept which presupposes that of identity is that of integrity. It can be dealt with briefly because integrity simply means a willingness not to violate one's identity, in the many ways in which such violation is possible.

---

[18] There is no space within this short book to discuss in detail the difference between the concept of identity presented here and those presented by Erikson. I hope to publish a detailed discussion of this difference on another occasion.

Today the main temptations for violation of one's identity are the opportunities for advancement in industrial society. Since the life within the society tends to make man experience himself as a thing anyway, a sense of identity is a rare phenomenon. But the problem is complicated by the fact that aside from identity as a conscious phenomenon as described above, there is a kind of unconscious identity. By that I mean that some people, while consciously they have turned into things, carry unconsciously a sense of their identity precisely because the social process has not succeeded in transforming them completely into things. These people, when yielding to the temptation of violating their integrity, may have a sense of guilt which is unconscious and which gives them a feeling of uneasiness, although they are not aware of its cause. It is all too easy for orthodox psychoanalytic procedure to explain a sense of guilt as the result of one's incestuous wishes or one's "unconscious homosexuality." The truth is that inasmuch as a person is not entirely dead—in a psychological sense—he feels guilty for living without integrity.

Our discussion of identity and integrity needs to be supplemented by at least briefly mentioning another attitude for which Monsignor W. Fox has coined an excellent word: *vulnerability*. The person who experiences himself as an ego and whose sense of identity is that of ego-identity naturally wants to protect this thing —him, his body, memory, property, and so on, but also his opinions and emotional investments which have become part of his ego. He is constantly on the defensive against anyone or any experience which could disturb the permanence and solidity of his mummified existence. In contrast, the person who experiences himself not as having but as being permits himself to be vulnerable. Nothing belongs to him except that he *is* by being alive. But at every moment in which he loses his sense of activity, in which he is unconcentrated, he is in danger of neither having anything nor being anybody. This danger he can meet only by constant alertness, awakeness, and aliveness, and he is vulnerable compared with the ego-man, who is safe because he *has* without *being.*

I would speak now of hope, faith, and courage as other "humane experiences," but having treated them extensively in the first chapter, I can forgo any further reference at this point.

This discussion of all the phenomena of "humane experiences" would remain utterly incomplete without making explicit the phenomenon which implicitly underlies the concepts discussed here: *transcendence.* Transcendence is customarily used in a religious context and it refers to transcending the human dimensions in order to arrive at the experience of the divine. Such definition of transcendence makes good sense in a theistic system; from a nontheistic standpoint it can be said that the concept of God was a poetic symbol for the act of leaving the prison of one's ego and achieving the freedom of openness and relatedness to the world. If we speak of transcendence in a nontheological sense, there is no need for the concept of God. However, the psychological reality is the same. The basis for love, tenderness, compassion, interest, responsibility, and identity is precisely that of being versus having, *and that means* transcending the ego. It means letting go of one's ego, letting go of one's greed, making oneself empty in order to fill oneself, making oneself poor in order to be rich.

In our wish to survive physically, we obey the biological impulse imprinted on us since the birth of living substance and transmitted by millions of years of evolution. The wish to be alive "beyond survival" is the creation of man in history, his alternative to despair and failure.

This discussion of "humane experiences" culminates in the statement that *freedom* is a quality of being fully humane. Inasmuch as we transcend the realm of physical survival and inasmuch as we are not driven by fear, impotence, narcissism, dependency, etc., we transcend compulsion. Love, tenderness, reason, interest, integrity, and identity—they all are the children of freedom. Political freedom is a condition of human freedom only inasmuch as it furthers the development of what is specifically human. Political freedom in an alienated society, which contributes to the dehumanization of man, becomes un-freedom.

6. VALUES AND NORMS

Thus far we have not touched upon one of the fundamental elements of the human situation, and that is man's need for values which guide his actions and feelings. Of course, there is usually a discrepancy between what people consider their values to be and the effective values which direct them and of which they are not aware. In the industrial society, the official, conscious values are those of the religious and humanistic tradition: individuality, love, compassion, hope, etc. But these values have become ideologies for most people and are not effective in motivating human behavior. The unconscious values which directly motivate human behavior are those which are generated in the social system of the bureaucratic, industrial society, those of property, consumption, social position, fun, excitement, etc. This discrepancy between conscious and ineffective and unconscious and effective values creates havoc within the personality. Having to act differently from what he has been taught and professes to abide by makes man feel guilty, distrustful of himself and others. It is that very discrepancy which our young generation has spotted and against which it has taken such an uncompromising stand.

Values—the official or the factual ones—are not unstructuralized items but form a hierarchy in which certain supreme values determine the others as necessary correlates to the realization of the former. The development of those specifically human experiences which we have just discussed form the system of values within the psychospiritual tradition of the West and of India and China during the last 4,000 years. As long as these values rested upon revelation, they were binding for those who believed in the source of revelation, which means, as far as the West is concerned, in God. (The values of Buddhism and Taoism were not based on revelation by a superior being. Specifically, in Buddhism, the validity of values is derived from an examination of the basic human condition—suffering, the recognition of its source, i.e., greed, and the recognition of the ways to overcome greed, i.e., the "eightfold path." For this reason, the Buddhist hierarchy of values is accessible to anyone who does not have any premise except that of rational thought and authentic human experience.) For those in the West, the question arises whether the hierarchy of values presented by Western religion can have any foundation other than that of revelation by God.

Summing up briefly, we find among those who do not accept God's authority as the foundation of values the following patterns:

1. Complete relativism which claims that all values are matters of personal taste and have no foundation beyond such taste. Sartre's philosophy basically does not differ from this relativism, since man's freely chosen project can be anything and hence a supreme value, as long as it is authentic.

2. Another concept of values is that of socially immanent values. The defenders of this position start with the premise that the survival of each society with its own social structure and contradictions must be the supreme goal for all its members and hence that those norms which are conducive to the survival of that par-

ticular society are the highest values and are binding for each individual. In this view, ethical norms are identical with social norms and social norms serve the perpetuation of any given society—including its injustices and contradictions. It is obvious that the elite which governs a society uses all the means at its disposal to make the social norms on which its power rests appear to be sacred, universal norms, either revealed by God or inherent in human nature.

3. Another value concept is that of biologically immanent values. The reasoning of some of the representatives of this thought is that experiences like love, loyalty, group solidarity are rooted in corresponding feelings in the animal: human love and tenderness are seen as having their roots in the animal mother's attitude toward its young, solidarity as rooted in the group cohesion among many animal species. This point of view has much to be said for it, but it does not answer the critical question of the difference between human tenderness, solidarity, and other "humane experiences" and those observed in the animal. The analogies which authors like Konrad Lorenz present are far from convincing. Biologically immanent value systems often arrive at results which are the very opposite of the humanist-oriented one discussed here. In a well-known type of social Darwinism, egotism, competition, and aggressiveness are conceived as the highest values because they are allegedy the main principles on which survival and evolution of the species rest.

The value system corresponding to the point of view presented in this book is based on the concept of what Albert Schweitzer called "reverence for life." Valuable or good is all that which contributes to the greater unfolding of man's specific faculties and furthers life. Negative or bad is everything that strangles life and paralyzes man's activeness. All norms of the great humanist religions like Buddhism, Judaism, Christianity, or Islam or the great humanist philosophers from the pre-Socratics to contemporary thinkers are the specific elaboration of this general principle of values. Overcoming of one's greed, love for one's neighbor, knowledge of the truth (different from the uncritical knowledge of facts) are the goals common to all humanist philosophical and religious systems of the West and the East. Man could discover these values only when he had reached a certain social and economic development which left him enough time and energy to enable him to think exclusively beyond the aims of mere physical survival. But since this point has been reached, these values have been upheld and, to some extent, practiced within the most disparate societies—from thinkers in the Hebrew tribes to the philosophers of the Greek city-states and the Roman Empire, theologians in the medieval feudal society, thinkers in the Renaissance, the philosophers of the Enlightenment, down to such thinkers of the industrial society as Goethe, Marx, and, in our age, Einstein and Schweitzer. There is no doubt that in this phase of industrial society, the practice of these values becomes more and more difficult, precisely because the reified man experiences little of life and instead follows principles which have been programed for him by the machine.

Any real hope for victory over the dehumanized society of the megamachine and for the building up of a humanist industrial society rests upon the condition that the values of the tradition are brought to life, and that a society emerges in which love and integrity are possible.

Having stated that the values I have called humanistic deserve respect and consideration because of the fact that they represent a consensus among all higher forms of culture, I must ask the question whether there is objective, scientific evidence which could make it compelling, or at least highly suggestive, that these are the norms which should motivate our private lives and which should be guiding principles for all the social enterprises and activities we plan.

Referring to what I have said earlier in this chapter, I submit that the validity of norms is based on the conditions of human existence. Human personality constitutes a system with one minimal requirement: avoidance of madness. But once this requirement is fulfilled, man has choices: He can devote his life to hoarding or to producing, to loving or hating, to being or having, etc. Whatever he chooses, he builds a structure (his character) in which certain orientations are dominant and others necessarily follow. The laws of human existence by no means lead to the postulation of *one* set of values as the only possible one. They lead to alternatives and we have to decide which of the alternatives are superior to others.

But are we not begging the issue by speaking of "superior" norms? Who decides what is superior? The answer to this question will be made easier if we begin with some concrete alternatives: If man is deprived of his freedom, he will become either resigned and lose vitality, or furious and aggressive. If he is bored, he will become passive or indifferent to life. If he is cut down to an IBM-card equivalent, he will lose his originality, creativeness, and interests. If I maximize certain factors, I minimize others correspondingly.

The question then arises, which of these possibilities seems preferable: the alive, joyful, interested, active, peaceful structure or the unalive, dull, uninterested, passive, aggressive structure.

What matters is to recognize that we deal with structures and cannot pick out preferred parts from one structure and combine them with preferred parts of the other structure. The fact of structuralization in social as well as in individual life narrows down our choice to that between structures, rather than that between single traits, alone or combined. Indeed, what most people would like is to be aggressive, competitive, maximally successful in the market, liked by everybody and at the same time tender, loving, and a person of integrity. Or, on the social level, people would like a society which maximizes material production and consumption, military and political power and at the same time furthers peace, culture, and spiritual values. Such ideas are unrealistic, and usually the "nice" human features in the mixture serve to dress up or hide the ugly features. Once one recognizes that the choice is between various structures and sees clearly which structures are "real possibilities," the difficulty in choosing becomes greatly reduced and little doubt remains which value structure one prefers. Persons with different character structures will be in favor of the respective value system which appeals to their character. Thus, the biophilous, life-loving person will decide for biophilous values, and the necrophilous person for necrophilous ones. Those who are in between will try to avoid a clear choice, or eventually make a choice according to the dominant forces in their character structure.

Nothing much would be gained practically if one could prove on objective grounds that one value structure is superior to all others; for those who do not agree with the "superior" value structure because it contradicts the demands rooted in their character structure, objective proof would not be compelling.

Nevertheless, I want to submit, mainly for theoretical reasons, that one may arrive at objective norms if one starts with one premise: that it is desirable that a living system should grow and produce the maximum of vitality and intrinsic harmony, that is, subjectively, of well-being. An examination of the system Man can show that the biophilous norms are more conducive to the growth and strength of the system while the necrophilous norms are conducive to dysfunction and pathology. The validity of the norms would follow from their function in promoting the optimum of growth and well-being and the minimum of ill-being.

Empirically, most people waver between various systems of values, and hence never fully develop in the one or the other direction. They have neither great virtues nor great vices. They are, as Ibsen has so beautifully expressed it in *Peer Gynt,* like a coin whose stamp has been worn away; the person has no self and no identity, but is afraid to make this discovery.

Chapter V

Steps to the Humanization of Technological Society

1. GENERAL PREMISES

If we are now to consider the possibility of humanizing the industrial society as it has developed in the second Industrial Revolution, we must begin by considering those institutions and methods which for economic as well as psychological reasons cannot be done away with without the total disruption of our society. These elements are: (1) The large-scale centralized enterprise as it has developed in the last decades in government, business, universities, hospitals, etc. This process of centralization is still continuing, and soon almost all major purposeful activities will be carried on by large systems. (2) Large-scale planning within each system, which results from the centralization. (3) Cybernation, that is cybernetics and automation, as the major theoretical and practical principle of control, with the computer as the most important element in automation.

But not only these three elements are here to stay. There is another element which appears in all social systems: the system Man. As I pointed out earlier, this does not mean that human nature is not malleable; it means that it allows only a limited number of potential structures, and confronts us with certain ascertainable alternatives. The most important alternative as far as the technological society is concerned is the following: if man is passive, bored, unfeeling, and one-sidedly cerebral, he develops pathological symptoms like anxiety, depression, depersonalization, indifference to life, and violence. Indeed, as Robert H. Davis wrote in a penetrating paper, ". . . the long-range implications of a cybernated world for mental health are disturbing." [1] It is important to stress this point, since most planners deal with the human factor as one which could adapt itself to any condition without causing any disturbances.

The possibilities which confront us are few and ascertainable. One possibility is that we continue in the direction we have taken. This would lead to such disturbances of the total system that either thermonuclear war or severe human pathology would be the outcome. The second possibility is the attempt to change that direction by force or violent revolution. This would lead to the breakdown of the whole system and violence and brutal dictatorship as a result. The third possibility is the humanization of the system, in such a way that it serves the purpose of man's well-being and growth, or in other words, his life process. In this case, the central elements of the second Industrial Revolution will be kept intact. The question is, Can this be done and what steps need to be taken to achieve it?

I hardly need to assure the reader that it is not my intention to present a "plan," which would show how to achieve this end. Not only could that not be done in a short book; it would also require many studies which could be made only through the collaboration of competent and concerned people. My intention is to discuss the steps which, to me, are the most important ones: (1) Planning which includes the system Man and which is based on norms which follow from the examination of the optimal functioning of the human being. (2) Activation of the individual by methods of grass-roots activity and responsibility, by changing the present methods of alienated bureaucracy into one of humanistic man-

---

[1] "The Advance of Cybernation: 1965–1985," in *The Guaranteed Income*, ed. by Robert Theobald (New York: Doubleday Anchor Books, 1967).

agement. (3) Changing of the consumption pattern in the direction of consumption that contributes to activation and discourages "passivation." [2] (4) The emergence of new forms of psychospiritual orientation and devotion, which are equivalents of the religious systems of the past.

2. HUMANISTIC PLANNING

Continuing the discussion about planning begun in Chapter III, I wish to state again that all planning is directed by value judgments and norms, whether the planners are aware of it or not. This holds true also of all computer planning; both the selection of facts which are fed into the computer as well as the programing imply value judgments. If I want to maximize economic output, my facts as well as my program differ from what they would be if I wanted to maximize human well-being, in terms of joy, interest in work, etc. In the latter case other facts are considered and the program is different.

Several serious questions arise here: How can one have any knowledge about human values except by accepting the traditional ones, which at least have the validation of consensus or are accepted as a matter of personal taste or bias? In Chapter IV, I have referred to the fact that the state of well-being of man can be described as empirically and objectively as the state of ill-being; conditions conducive to well-being can be ascertained, as can those leading to ill-being, both physical and mental. A study of the system Man can lead to the acceptance of objectively valid values, on

---

[2] I coin this word in parallel to activation; while it is not to be found in the dictionary, it is a necessary word because there are some circumstances which make man more active and others which make him more passive.

the grounds that they lead to the optimal functioning of the system or, at least, that if we realize the possible alternatives, the humanist norms would be accepted as preferable to their opposites by most sane people.

Whatever the merits of the source of the validity of humanist norms, the general aim of a humanized industrial society can be thus defined: the change of the social, economic, and cultural life of our society in such a way that it stimulates and furthers the growth and aliveness of man rather than cripples it; that it activates the individual rather than making him passive and receptive; that our technological capacities serve man's growth. If this is to be, we must regain control over the economic and social system; man's will, guided by his reason, and by his wish for optimal aliveness, must make the decisions.

Given these general aims, what is the procedure of humanistic planning? *Computers should become a functional part in a life-oriented social system and not a cancer which begins to play havoc and eventually kills the system.* Machines or computers must become means for ends which are determined by man's reason and will. The values which determine the selection of facts and which influence the programing of the computer must be gained on the basis of the knowledge of human nature, its various possible manifestations, its optimal forms of development, and the real needs conducive to this development. That is to say, man, not technique, must become the ultimate source of values; optimal human development and not maximal production the criterion for all planning.[3]

---

[3] Hasan Ozbekhan has formulated the problem very succinctly: "What we have failed to do in all this is to ascribe operational meaning to the so-called desirables that motivate us, to question their intrinsic worth, to assess the long-range consequences of our aspirations and actions, to wonder whether the outcome we seem to be expecting does in fact correspond to that *quality of life* we say we are striving for—and whether our current actions will lead us there. In other words, in this writer's

Aside from this, planning in the field of economics must be extended to the whole system; furthermore, the system Man must be integrated into the whole social system. Man, as the planner, must be aware of the role of man as part of the whole system. Just as man is the only case of life being aware of itself, man as a system builder and analyzer must make himself the object of the system he analyzes. *This means that the knowledge of man, his nature, and the real possibilities of its manifestations must become one of the basic data for any social planning.*

What has been said thus far about planning was based on the theoretical assumption that the planners were essentially determined by their wish for the optimal welfare of society and the individuals which make it up. But, unfortunately, in practice such an assumption cannot be made. (I am, of course, not speaking about the *ideas* planners have about their own motivations. They, like most men, believe their motives to be rational and moral. Most men need to have such rationalizations [ideologies] for their actions partly in order to support themselves by the feeling of moral righteousness, partly in order to deceive others about their real motivations.) On the level of government planning, the personal interests of the politicians often interfere with their integrity and hence with their capacity for humanist planning. This danger can be reduced only by a much more active participation of the citizen in the decision-making process, and by finding ways and methods by which government planning is controlled by those for whom the planning is done.[4]

Should then government planning be further reduced

---

conception of planning we are in the deeper sense failing to plan." (Cf. the article by Hasan Ozbekhan, *op. cit.* I also gratefully acknowledge the suggestions I received by subsequent personal communication from Mr. Ozbekhan; furthermore, from Martin K. Starr and Raymond G. Brown.)

[4] More about this follows later on in this chapter.

and most planning, including that in the public sector, be left to the big corporations? The arguments for this idea are that the big corporations are not burdened with outmoded procedures and are not dependent on fluctuating political pressures; that they are more advanced in system analysis, immediate application of research to technique; and that they are guided by men who have more objectivity because they do not have to fight every few years in election campaigns for their right to continue their work. Most importantly, management and system analysis being now one of the most advanced types of activities, it stands to reason that it will attract many of the most advanced minds, not only in terms of intelligence but also in terms of a vision of human well-being. These and many other arguments are very persuasive but not convincing with regard to two crucial points: First, the corporation operates for profit, and its interest in profit, although very modified in comparison with the profit interest of the nineteenth-century entrepreneur, often interferes with the best interests of the community. Second, the private corporation is not even subject to that small control to which government is subject in a democratic system. (If one would object to this by saying that the corporation is controlled by the market, i.e., indirectly by the consumer, one would ignore the fact that the tastes and desires of the consumer are largely manipulated by the corporation.) To believe in the wisdom and good will of the management is not a sufficient guarantee that the majority might not plan in accordance with impersonal technical feasibility rather than for the sake of human development. Precisely because the more conventionally minded managers do not lack good will, but rather imagination and vision of a fully human life, they are even more dangerous, from the standpoint of humanistic planning. In fact, their personal decency makes them more immune to doubts about the methods of their planning. For these reasons, I do not share the optimism expressed by John Kenneth Galbraith and others. I propose that corporation planning also should be subject to controls, by the government and by independent bodies of those who are subjects of their planning.[5]

3. ACTIVATION AND LIBERATION OF ENERGIES

It follows, from all that has been said in the previous chapters about man, that one basic requirement for his well-being is to be active, in the sense of the productive exercise of all his faculties; that one of the most pathogenic features in our society is the trend to make man passive, by depriving him of the chance of active participation in the affairs of his society, in the enterprise in which he works, and, in fact, although more hidden, in his personal affairs. This "passivation" of man is partly due to the "alienated bureaucratic" method used in all centralized enterprises.

Humanistic versus Alienated Bureaucratic Method

Here, as so often, people are confronted by a confusing false dichotomy. They believe that the choice is between an anarchic system without any organization and control and, on the other hand, the kind of bureaucracy which is typical both for contemporary industrialism and even more so for the Soviet system. But this alternative is by no means the only one, and we have other options. The option I have in mind is that between

---

[5] Classic socialism thought that this problem could be solved only by the socialization (nationalization) of the big enterprises. But aside from the fact that in the United States such a step is politically not feasible, it is also questionable as a real solution to the problem. As the example of the Soviet Union shows, the state-appointed managers may make their decisions in terms of the same efficiency and material output criteria as those of the private corporation. What matters are the values which guide the planning, and the degree of control from below.

the "humanistic bureaucratic" or "humanistic management" [6] method and the "alienated bureaucratic"
method by which we conduct our affairs.

This alienated bureaucratic procedure can be characterized in several ways. First of all, it is a one-way
system; orders, suggestions, planning emanate from the
top and are directed to the bottom of the pyramid.
There is no room for the individual's initiative. Persons
are "cases," whether welfare cases or medical cases, or,
whatever the frame of reference is, cases which can all
be put down on a computer card without those individual features which designate the difference between a
"person" and a "case."

Our bureaucratic method is irresponsible, in the sense
that it does not "respond" to the needs, views, requirements of an individual. This irresponsibility is closely
related to the case-character of the person who becomes
an "object" of the bureaucracy. One cannot respond to
a *case* but one can respond to a *person*. This irresponsibility of the bureaucrat has another aspect which has
been a feature of bureaucracy for a long time. The
bureaucrat, feeling himself part of the bureaucratic machine, most of all wishes not to take responsibility, that
is to say, to make decisions for which he could be
criticized. He tries to avoid making any decisions which
are not clearly formulated by his case rules and, if in
doubt, he sends the person to another bureaucrat who,
in turn, does the same. Anyone who has dealt with a
bureaucratic organization knows this process of being
sent around from one bureaucrat to the other and,
sometimes after much effort, coming out at the same
door which he had entered without ever having been
listened to except in the peculiar way in which bureaucrats listen, sometimes pleasantly, sometimes im-

---

[6] In the following pages, I shall use the term "humanistic
management" instead of "humanistic bureaucracy," because the
word "bureaucracy" itself is often understood to refer to an
alienated type of system.

patiently, but almost always with an attitude which is a mixture of their own helplessness, irresponsibility, and sense of superiority toward the "petitioning" subject. Our bureaucratic method gives the individual the feeling that there is nothing which he can initiate and organize without the help of the bureaucratic machine. As a result, it paralyzes initiative and creates a deep sense of impotence.

What Is the Nature of "Humanistic Management" and Its Methods?

The basic principle of the humanistic management method is that, in spite of the bigness of the enterprises, centralized planning, and cybernation, the individual participant asserts himself toward the managers, circumstances, and machines, and ceases to be a powerless particle which has no active part in the process. Only by such affirmation of his will can the energies of the individual be liberated and his mental balance be restored.

The same principle of humanistic management can also be expressed in this way: While in alienated bureaucracy all power flows from above downward, in humanistic management there is a two-way street; the "subjects" [7] of the decision made above respond according to their own will and concerns; their response not only reaches the top decision makers but forces them to respond in turn. The "subjects" of decision making have a right to challenge the decision makers. Such a challenge would first of all require a rule that if a sufficient number of "subjects" demanded that the corresponding bureaucracy (on whatever level) answer questions, explain its procedures, the decision makers would respond to the demand.

At this point, so many objections to the foregoing

---

[7] In the following, I shall call those subject to control by bureaucracy "subjects."

suggestions will have accumulated in the mind of the reader that I had better discuss them right here if I do not want to lose the reader's attention for what follows in this chapter. I deal first with the management of enterprises.

The first objection probably is that the type of active participation of the "subjects" would be incompatible with efficient centralized management and planning. This objection is plausible (a) provided one does not have any compelling reason to think that the present method of alienated bureaucracy is pathogenic; (b) if one thinks only of the tried and proven methods and shies away from imaginative new solutions; (c) if one insists that even if one could find new methods, the principle of maximal efficiency must never be given up even for a time. If, on the other hand, one follows the considerations offered in this book and recognizes the grave danger for the total system of our society inherent in our bureaucratic methods, these objections are not as compelling as they are to those who are satisfied with the operation of our present system.

More specifically, if one recognizes the difficulties and does not start out with the conviction that they are unsurmountable, one will begin to examine the problems concretely and in detail. Here, too, one may arrive at the conclusion that the dichotomy between maximal centralization and complete decentralization presents an unnecessary polarization, that one can deal with the concept of *optimal* centralization and *optimal* grass-roots participation. Optimal centralization would be the degree of centralization which is necessary for effective large-scale organization and planning; optimal participation would be the participation which does not make centralized management impossible, yet permits the participants the optimum of responsible participation. This formulation is obviously rather general and not sufficient as a basis for taking immediate steps. If a problem of such magnitude emerges in the application of scientific knowledge to technique, the engineer is not discouraged; he recognizes the necessity of research which will result in the solution of the problem. But as soon as we deal with human problems, such difficulties tend to discourage most people or they flatly state that "it cannot be done."

We have, indeed, an unbounded imagination and initiative for solving technical problems, but a most restricted imagination when we deal with human problems. Why is this so? An obvious answer is that we do not have the knowledge in the field of the science of man that we have in the natural sciences and in technique. But this answer is not convincing; why don't we have the necessary knowledge? Or, and this is even more to the point, why don't we apply the knowledge we do have? Nothing can be *proved* without further study, but I am convinced that to find a practical solution for the integration of optimal centralization and optimal decentralization will be less difficult than to find technical solutions for space travel. The real answer why this kind of research is not done lies in the fact that, considering our present priorities, our interest in finding humanely more acceptable solutions to our social organization is only feeble. Nevertheless, while emphasizing the need for research, we must not forget that there has already been a good deal of experimentation and discussion about these problems going on in the last decades. Both in the field of industrial psychology and management science, one finds a number of valuable theoretical discussions and experiments.

Another objection, often combined with the previous one, says that as long as there is an effective control of decision making on the political level, there is no need for active participation in a corporation, since it will be properly supervised by the legislative and executive branches of the government. This objection does not take into account the fact that today government and the corporations are already so interwoven that it is difficult to say who controls whom—furthermore, that government decisions themselves are not under effective

control by the citizens. But even if there existed a satisfactory active participation of the citizens in the political
process, as it is suggested here, the corporation itself
must become responsive to the will, not only of the
participants, but of the public at large inasmuch as it
is affected by the decisions of the corporation. If such
direct control over the corporation does not exist, it
will be very difficult for the government to exercise
power over the private sector of the system.

Another objection will point out that the double responsibility in decision making which is proposed here
will be a source of endless friction between the top and the
"subjects" and will be ineffective for this psychological
reason. Talking about the problem in an abstract sense,
we may easily find it formidable, but once such changes
are accepted, the resulting conflicts will be far less
sharp and insoluble than they are if one looks at the
picture in an abstract way. After all, the managers have
an interest in performing, and so have the participants
in an enterprise. As soon as the bureaucrat becomes
"vulnerable," that is to say, begins to respond to desires
and claims from those subject to him, both sides will
become more interested in the problems than in preserving their positions either as authority or challenger.
That this is possible has been shown at a number of
universities in the United States and abroad where once
the participation of students was accepted, there was
little friction between administration and students. This
has been demonstrated in the Yugoslav system of the
self-management of the workers and in the experience
of the many cooperative movements all over the world.

If the bureaucratic mode were changed from an
alienated to a humanistic one, it would necessarily lead
to a change in the type of manager who is successful.
The defensive type of personality who clings to his bureaucratic image and who is afraid of being vulnerable
and of confronting persons directly and openly would be
at a disadvantage. On the other hand, the imaginative,

nonfrightened, responsive person would be successful if the method of management were changed. These considerations show how erroneous it is to speak of certain methods of management which cannot be changed because the managers "would not be willing or capable of changing them." What is left out here is the fact that new methods would constitute a selective principle for managers. This does not mean that most present managers would be replaced by the new type of manager. No doubt there are many who under the present system cannot utilize their responsive capacities and who will be able to do so once the system gives them a chance.

Among the objections to the idea of active participation of the individual in the enterprises in which he works, perhaps the most popular one is the statement that, in view of increasing cybernation, the working time of the individual will be so short and the time devoted to leisure so long that the activation of the individual will no longer need to take place in his work situation, but will be sufficiently accomplished during his leisure time. This idea, I believe, is based on an erroneous concept of human existence and of work. Man, even under the most favorable technological conditions, has to take the responsibility of producing food, clothing, housing, and all other material necessities. This means he has to work. Even if most physical labor is taken over by the machines, man has still to take part in the process of the exchange between himself and nature; only if man were a disembodied being or an angel with no physical needs, would work completely disappear. Man, being in need of assimilating nature, of organizing and directing the process of material production, of distribution, of social organization, of responses to natural catastrophes, can never sit back and let things take care of themselves. Work in a technological society may not be a "curse" any more, but that paradisiacal state in which man does not have to take care of his material needs is a technological fantasy. Or will the solution be, as

Brzezinski [8] predicts, that only the elite will have the privilege of working while the majority is busy with consumption? Indeed, that could be a solution to the problem, but it would reduce the majority to the status of slaves, in the paradoxical sense that they would become irresponsible and useless parasites, while the free man alone would have the right to live a full life, which includes work. *If man is passive in the process of production and organization, he will also be passive during his leisure time.* If he abdicates responsibility and participation in the process of sustaining life, he will acquire the passive role in all other spheres of life and be dependent on those who take care of him. We already see this happening today. Man has more leisure time than before, but most people show this passiveness in the leisure which is forced upon them by the method of alienated bureaucratism. Leisure time is mostly of the spectator or consumption type; rarely is it an expression of activeness.

One example may clarify the point I am trying to make, that of taking care of one's health. It seems quite feasible that many functions of the art of medicine can be taken over by the computer, like diagnosis, treatment, prescription, etc. But it appears doubtful that the capacity for highly individualized observation, which the outstanding physician has, can be replaced by the computer, e.g., observation of the expression in a person's eye or face, a capacity impossible to quantify and to translate into programing language. Outstanding achievements in medicine will be lost in a completely automatized system.[9] But beyond this, the individual will be so completely conditioned to submit to machines that he

---

[8] *Op. cit.*

[9] Just as the computer chess player is better than the average chess player but not as good as the chess master, or as the computer can be programed to compose music à la Mozart or Beethoven without ever reaching the qualities of a Mozart or Beethoven composition.

will lose the capacity to take care of his health in an active, responsible way. He will run to the "health service" whenever he has a physical problem, and he will lose the ability to observe his own physical processes, to discern changes, and to consider remedies for himself, even simple ones of keeping a diet or doing the right kind of exercise.

If man should be relieved of the task of being responsible for the functioning of the productive and administrative system, he would become a being of complete helplessness, lack of self-confidence, and dependence on the machine and its specialists; he would not only be incapable of making active use of his leisure time, he would also face a catastrophe whenever the smooth functioning of the system was threatened.

In this respect one more point, and a very important one, must be mentioned. Even if machines could take care of all work, of all planning, of all organizational decisions, and even of all health problems, they cannot take care of the problems arising between man and man. In this sphere of interpersonal relations, human judgment, response, responsibility and decision the machine cannot replace human functioning. There are those, like Marcuse, who think that in a cybernated and "non-repressive" society that is completely satisfied materially there would be no more human conflicts like those expressed in the Greek or Shakespearean drama or the great novels. I can understand that completely alienated people can see the future of human existence in this way, but I am afraid they express more about their own emotional limitations than about future possibilities. The assumption that the problems, conflicts, and tragedies between man and man will disappear if there are no materially unfulfilled needs is a childish daydream.

Active participation in the affairs of the country as a whole and of states and communities, as well as of large enterprises, would require the formation of face-to-face groups, within which the process of information exchange, debate, and decision making would be conducted. Before discussing the structure of such groups in all kinds of centralized enterprises and political decision making, respectively, let us have a look at the characteristics such face-to-face groups should have.

The first is that the *number* of participating people must be restricted in such a way that the discussion remains direct and does not allow the rhetoric or the manipulating influence of demagogues to become effective. If people meet regularly and know each other, they begin to feel whom they can trust and whom they cannot, who is constructive and who is not, and in the process of their own participation, their own sense of responsibility and self-confidence grows.

Second, objective and relevant *information* which is the basis for everyone's having an approximately clear and accurate picture of the basic issues must be given to each group.

The problem of adequate information presents many difficulties which force us into some digressions. Are the issues with which we deal in foreign and domestic policy or in the management of a corporation not so intricate and specialized that only the highly trained specialist can understand them? If that were so, we would have to admit that the democratic process in the traditional sense of the citizen's participation in decision making is not feasible any more; we would have to admit, furthermore, that the constitutional function of Congress is also outmoded. The individual senator or representative certainly does not have the specialized knowledge which is assumed to be necessary. The president himself does seem to be dependent on the advice of a group of highly trained specialists, since he is not supposed to understand problems of such intricacy that they are outside the grasp of an informed and educated citizen. Briefly, if the assumption of the insurmountable complexity and difficulty of the data were correct, the democratic process would be an empty form, covering up government by technicians. The same would hold true in the process of management also. If top managers could not understand the highly complex technical problems they are called upon to decide, they would simply have to accept the decisions of their technical experts.

The idea that the data have become so difficult and complex that only highly specialized experts can tackle them is largely influenced by the fact that in the natural sciences such a degree of specialization has been reached that often only a few scientists are capable of fully understanding the work of a colleague in their own field. Fortunately, most data which are necessary for the decision making in politics and management are not of the same order of difficulty or specialization. In fact, computerization reduces the difficulties because it can construct different models and show different outcomes according to the premises which are used in the programing. Let us look at the example of American foreign policy in reference to the Soviet bloc. One's judgment depends on one's analysis of the plans and intentions of the Soviet bloc, their goals and flexibility in the pursuit of their goals, especially as it is dependent on their wish to avoid catastrophes. The same, of course, holds true for American, Chinese, German, etc., foreign policy, also on the plans and intentions of American foreign policy as it is or can be understood by the opponent. I submit that the basic facts are accessible to anyone who keeps himself informed by reading all the available news. (It is true that only a few newspapers, like *The New York Times*, give all the necessary information, and even those sometimes with a biased selection; but that could be remedied and does not touch the essential issue.) On the basis of the facts, the informed, thoughtful, and critical citizen is capable of getting the basic information which he needs to form a picture of the fundamental issues.

It is widely believed that since we lack access to secret information, our information is woefully inadequate. I believe that this view overestimates the importance of secret information, not to speak of the fact that the data which secret intelligence offers are often plainly erroneous, as in the case of the invasion of Cuba. Most of the information one needs in order to understand the intentions of other countries can be gained by a thorough and rational analysis of their structure and their record, provided that the analysts are not biased by their own emotions. Some of the best analyses of the Soviet Union, China, the origins of the cold war, etc., can be found in the work of the scholars who had no secret information at their disposal. The fact is that the less one trusts the penetrating and critical analysis of the data, the more one demands secret information, which often is a poor substitute for analysis. I am not denying that there is a problem; secret military intelligence that informs the top decision makers about questions like new missile sites, nuclear explosions, etc., can be of importance; yet if one has an adequate picture of the other country's aims and constraints, often such information, and especially its evaluation, is secondary to the general analysis. The point of this argument is not to say that secret information has no importance, but that a thorough critical analysis of the available data makes it possible to have a basis for informed judgment. It should be added that it is an open question whether there is a real need to keep as much information secret as the political and military bureaucracies want us to believe. First of all, the need for secrecy corresponds to the wishes of the bureaucracy. It helps support a hierarchy of various levels, characterized by their access to various kinds of security classification. It also enhances their power, for in every group, from primitive tribes to a complex bureaucracy, the possession of secrets makes the owners of the secrets appear to be endowed with a special magic, and hence superior to the average man. But aside from these considerations, it must be seriously questioned whether the advantages of some secret information (both sides know that some of their "secrets" are known to each other anyway) is worth the social effect of undermining the confidence of the citizen and all members of the legislature and executive—with the exception of the very few who have access to "top secrets"—in order to fulfill their decision-making roles. It may turn out that the military and diplomatic advantages gained by secrecy are smaller than the losses to our democratic system.

Returning from this digression to the problem of information in face-to-face groups, we must ask (a) how the necessary information can be transmitted to the group for which it is relevant and (b) how our education can increase the student's capacity for critical thought rather than to make of him a consumer of information. It would not be useful to go into details of how this type of information can be transmitted. Given sufficient concern and interest, there are no great obstacles to developing adequate methods.

A second requirement for the functioning of all face-to-face groups is *debate*. Through the increasing mutual knowledge of the members, the debate will lose an acrimonious and slogan-throwing character and will become a *dialogue* between human beings instead of a disputation. While there will always be fanatics and more or less sick as well as stupid people who cannot participate in this kind of debate, an atmosphere can be created which, without any force, eliminates the effectiveness of such individuals within the group. It is essential for the possibility of a dialogue that each member of the group not only try to be less defensive and more open, but also that he try to understand what the other person means to say rather than the actual formulation he gives to his thought. In every fruitful dialogue, each participant must help the other to clarify his thought rather than to force him to defend formulations about which he may have his own doubts. Dialogue implies always mutual clarification and often even understanding the other better than one understands oneself.

Eventually, information and debate would remain sterile and impotent if the group did not have the right to make *decisions* and if these decisions were not translated into the real process of that social sector to which they belong. While it is true that in order to act, man has to think first, it is equally true that if man has no chance to act, his thinking withers and loses its strength.

It is impossible to give a blueprint of what decisions the face-to-face groups in enterprises should be called upon to make. It is obvious that the very process of information and debate has an educational influence and changes the people who participate in it. Hence, they are likely to make more wrong decisions in the beginning than after many years of practice. It follows that the area of decision making should grow while people learn how to think, to debate, and to make judgments. In the beginning their decisions might be restricted to the right to ask their respective bureaucrats to explain decisions, to give specific information which is desired, and the right to initiate plans, rules, laws for the consideration of the decision-making bodies. The next step would be the right to enforce reconsideration of decisions by a qualified majority. Eventually, the face-to-face groups would be entitled to vote on fundamental principles of action, while the detailed execution of their principles would remain essentially a matter for the management. The decision of the face-to-face groups would be integrated into the whole processes of decision making, implementing the principle of central planning by the principle of the "subjects'" control and initiative. The consumer should also be represented in the decision-making process.

The development of trade unions in manufacturing industries represented a step in this direction. Events in recent decades have unfortunately turned these organizations away from their original broad social purposes. Today they provide a measure of workers' control over internal conditions; however, their sphere of action often does not extend much beyond wages, hours, and certain work practices. Furthermore, they all too often have developed along dehumanized bureaucratic lines and need to reorganize themselves if they are to fulfill their commitment to full membership participation.

To give some examples of fundamental problems which should be discussed in the face-to-face groups: In a factory, for instance, the participants would discuss the basic problems about which decisions have to be made: course of production, changes in techniques of production, working conditions, housing for participants, supervision of workers or employees, etc. The various possible courses of action would have to be mapped out, and the arguments in favor or against each of these alternatives made explicit.

The participant face-to-face group should become part of all enterprises, whether in business, or education, or health. The participant groups would operate within the various departments of the enterprise and be concerned with the problems of their particular department. As far as discussions referring to the enterprise as a whole are concerned, they could take place within all groups, whose decisions would be tallied. Again, there is no point in proposing details for this kind of organization since the working out of details requires a great deal of experimentation.

What holds true of participation in all kinds of enterprises holds true for political life too. In the modern national state with its size and complexity, the idea of expressing popular will has deteriorated to a competition between various parties and professional politicians, most of whom, at election time, tailor their program to what the polls say will gain them votes and when elected act according to various pressures brought to bear on them, of which the will of the voters is only one—but only a few according to their knowledge of the issues, their concern, and their conviction.

The fact is that there is a striking correlation between education and the political opinion of voters. The least informed voters lean more toward irrational, fanatical solutions, while the better educated ones show a tendency toward more realistic and rational solutions. Since, for many reasons, it is neither feasible nor desirable to restrict general suffrage in favor of the educated, and since the democratic form of society is superior to an authoritarian form which offers little hope that the philosophers will be kings, there is in the long run only one chance for the democratic process: to adapt it to the conditions of the twentieth century by a political process through which the voters become informed, interested, and concerned with the problems of their society, as the members of a Town Meeting were with the problems of their town. The development in communications techniques can become very helpful in this process.

Briefly, an equivalent of the Town Meeting which is feasible in a technological society could be the following: to form a kind of Lower House, composed of many thousands of groups of Town Meeting size, which would be well informed and debate and make decisions about principles of political actions; their decisions would form a new element in that of the existing systems of checks and balances; computer technique would allow a very fast process of tallying the decisions made by the participants in these Town Meetings. As political education grew they would become increasingly a part of the decision making on the national and state level. Because these meetings would be based on information and debate their decisions would be fundamentally different from those of a plebiscite or an opinion poll.

But a condition for even the possibility of these changes is that the power in the United States be returned to those organs which the Constitution has made responsible for the exercise of power in various areas. The military-industrial complex threatens to take over many functions of the legislative and executive branches. The Senate has lost a great deal of its constitutional role in influencing foreign policy (of which the courageous and imaginative efforts of Senator J. William Fulbright, Chairman of the Senate Foreign Relations Committee, has salvaged as much as was possible); the armed forces have become ever more influential in shaping of politics. Considering the size of our defense budget, it is not surprising that the Defense Department (and the CIA, operating without effective control by other branches of the governmental system) should tend to expand more and more. While this is understandable, it constitutes a crucial danger to our democratic system, a danger which can be averted only by the firm expression on the part of the voters of their intention of reasserting their will.[10]

Returning now from the problems of politics and economics to those of culture, we find that the change must be a similar one: from passive consumer culture to active, participant culture. This is not the place to go into details, but most readers will understand the difference between, for example, *spectator* art (similar to spectator sports) and *active* art, expressed in little theater groups, dancing, music, reading, and in other forms.

The very same question which exists with regard to spectator art versus active art applies to the sphere of teaching. Our educational system, whose façade is so impressive according to the number of students who go to college, is unimpressive in quality. Generally speaking, education has deteriorated to a tool for social advancement or, at best, into the use of knowledge for the practical application to the "food gathering" sector of human life. Even our teaching in liberal arts—while not done in the authoritarian style of the French system —is dispensed in an alienated and cerebral form. No wonder that the best minds of our college students are

---

[10] While revising this manuscript, I read the testimony of Vice-Admiral Hyman Rickover before the Senate Foreign Affairs Committee, who accused the Defense Department's civilian bureaucracy of creating foreign policy problems by financing and conducting behavioral and social science research abroad: "Given its vastly superior resources—the fact that even in peacetime it gets the major part of the taxes collected by the Federal government—the D.O.D. was bound to become the most influential of all the executive departments." (*New York Times,* July 19, 1968.)

literally "fed up" because they are fed, not stimulated. They are dissatisfied with the intellectual fare they get in most—although fortunately not in all—instances, and, in this mood, tend to discard all traditional writings, values, and ideas. It is futile simply to complain about this fact. One has to change its conditions, and this change can occur only if the split between emotional experience and thought is replaced by a new unity of heart and mind. This is not done by the method of reading the hundred great books—which is conventional and unimaginative. It can only be accomplished if the teachers themselves cease being bureaucrats hiding their own lack of aliveness behind their role of bureaucratic dispensers of knowledge; if they become—in a word, by Tolstoy—"the codisciples of their students." If the student does not become aware of the relevance of problems of philosophy, psychology, sociology, history, and anthropology to his own personal life and the life of his society, only the least gifted ones will pay attention to their courses. The result is that the apparent richness of our educational endeavor becomes an empty front which conceals a deep lack of response to the best cultural achievements of civilized history. The demands of students all over the world for greater participation in the administration of the universities and formulation of the curricula are only the more superficial symptoms of the demand for a different kind of education. If the educational bureaucracy does not understand this message, it will lose the respect which it receives from students and eventually that from the rest of the population. On the other hand, if it becomes "vulnerable," open and responsive to the interests of the students, it will sense the satisfaction and joy which meaningful activity carries with it as its reward.[11] This

---

[11] Marx expressed the nature of the nonbureaucratic influence over people succinctly in this way: "Let us assume *man* to be man, and his relationship to the world to be a human one. Then love can only be exchanged for love, trust for trust, etc.

humanism of education is, of course, not only that of higher education, but it starts with kindergarten and primary school. That this method can be applied even in the alphabetization of poor peasants and slum dwellers has been shown in the very successful methods of alphabetization devised and applied by Professor P. Freire in Brazil and now in Chile.

In concluding this discussion on participatory face-to-face groups, I urge the reader not to get stuck in the consideration of the merits of the detailed proposals I have made. They were made only as illustrations of the principle of the idea of participation, not because I think that any of the proposed suggestions in itself offers the best solution. To write in detail about the various possibilities for the formation of participatory groups would require at least another volume, which would be only one among many to be written by others on this subject.

Proposing methods of activation by participation aims at the revitalization of the democratic process. It is based on the conviction that American democracy must be strengthened and revitalized or it will wither away. It cannot remain static.

4. HUMANIZED CONSUMPTION

The aim of the activation of man in the technological

If you wish to enjoy art you must be an artistically cultivated person; if you wish to influence other people you must be a person who really has a stimulating and encouraging effect upon others. Every one of your relations to man and to nature must be a *specific expression,* corresponding to the object of your will, of your *real individual* life. If you love without evoking love in return, i.e., if you are not able, by the *manifestation* of yourself as a loving person, to make yourself a *beloved person,* then your love is impotent and a misfortune." For a correction of the distorted view of Marx as seeing man as mainly motivated by material greed, see my book *Marx's Concept of Man* (New York: Ungar Publishing Co., 1961). Cf. *The Symposium on Socialist Humanism,* ed. Erich Fromm (New York: Doubleday, 1965), and the writings of a large number of humanist Marxists in Europe and the United States, as well as in Yugoslavia, Czechoslovakia, Poland, and Hungary.

society requires another step as important and as difficult as replacement of the alienated bureaucratic structure by methods of humanist management. Again, I want to ask the reader to take the following proposals only as illustrations of desirable possibilities, not as definite aims and methods.

Up to the present, our industrial system has followed the principle that anything man wants or desires is to be accepted indiscriminately, and that if possible society should satisfy all of man's desires. We make a few exceptions to this principle; for instance, certain laws which restrict or even forbid the use of liquor regardless of a person's desire to drink as much as he likes; stronger ones against the taking of drugs, where even the possession of drugs like marijuana (the degree of whose harmfulness is still under debate) is penalized severely; we also restrict the sale and exhibition of so-called pornography. Furthermore, our laws forbid the sale of harmful food under the Food and Drug Act. In these areas, there is general consensus, crystallized in state and federal laws, that there are desires which are harmful to man and which should not be fulfilled in spite of the fact that a person craves for the satisfaction of these desires. While one can argue that so-called pornography does not constitute a real threat and, furthermore, that the *hidden* lasciviousness of our advertisements are at least as effective in arousing sexual cupidity as straight pornography would be, the principle is recognized that there are limits to the freedom of the satisfaction of subjective desires. Yet these restrictions are essentially based on only two principles: the concern for bodily harm, and the vestigial remnants of the Puritan morality. It is time we began to examine the whole problem of subjective needs and whether their *existence* is a sufficiently valid reason for their fulfillment; to question and examine the generally accepted principle of satisfying all needs—while never asking about their origins or effects.

In trying to find adequate solutions, we meet with two powerful obstacles. First, the interests of industry, whose imagination is fired by too many alienated men who cannot think of products which would help to make a human being more active rather than more passive. Besides this, industry knows that by advertising it can create needs and cravings which can be calculated in advance, so that there is little risk in losing profit if one continues the safe method of creating needs and selling the products which satisfy them.

The other difficulty lies in a certain concept of freedom which gains ever-increasing importance. The most important freedom in the nineteenth century was the freedom to use and invest property in any form which promised profit. Since managers of enterprises were at the same time the owners, their own acquisitive motivations made them emphasize this freedom of the use and investment of capital. In the middle of the twentieth century, most Americans do not own much property—even though there are a relatively large number of people who own large fortunes. The average American is employed and he is satisfied with relatively small savings, either in cash, stocks, bonds, or life insurance. For him, the freedom of investment of capital is a relatively minor issue; and even for most people who are able to buy stocks, this is a form of gambling in which they are counseled by investment advisers or simply trust the mutual investment funds. But the real feeling of freedom today lies in another sphere, in that of consumption. In this sphere, everybody except those who live a substandard existence experiences the *freedom of the consumer*.

Here is an individual who is powerless to have any influence—beyond a marginal one—on the affairs of the state or the enterprise in which he is employed. He has a boss, and his boss has a boss, and the boss of his boss has a boss, and there are very few individuals left who do not have a boss and do not obey the program of the managerial machine—of which they are a part. But what power does he have as a consumer? There are dozens of brands of cigarettes, toothpastes, soaps, deodorants, radios, television sets, movie and television programs, etc., etc. And they all woo his favor. They are all there "for his pleasure." He is free to favor the one against the other and he forgets that essentially there are no differences. This freedom to give his favors to his favorite commodity creates a sense of potency. The man who is impotent humanely becomes potent as a buyer and consumer. Can one make any attempt to restrict this sense of potency by restricting the freedom of choice in consumption? It seems reasonable to assume one can do so only under one condition, and that is that the whole climate of society changes and permits man to be more active and interested in his individual and social affairs, and hence less in need of that fake freedom to be the king in the supermarket.[12]

The attempt to question the pattern of unlimited consumption meets with another difficulty. Compulsive consumption compensates for anxiety. As I have indicated previously, the need for this type of consumption stems from the sense of inner emptiness, hopelessness, confusion, and tension. By "taking in" articles of consumption, the individual reassures himself that "he is," as it were. If consumption were to be reduced, a good deal of anxiety would become manifest. The resistance against the possible arousal of anxiety would result in an unwillingness to reduce consumption.

The most telling example of this mechanism is to be found in the public's attitude toward cigarette consumption. In spite of the well-known dangers to health, the majority goes on consuming cigarettes. Is it because they would rather take a chance of earlier death than

---

[12] A similar feeling of power exists in the voter who can choose from among the several candidates who woo his favor, or in the film-star fan who senses his power because he can make or break his idol.

forgo the pleasure? An analysis of the attitude of smokers shows that this is largely a rationalization. Cigarette consumption allays hidden anxiety and tension, and people would rather risk their health than to be confronted with their anxiety. Yet, once the quality of the process of living becomes more important than it is now, many people will stop smoking or overconsuming, not for the sake of their physical health but because only when they face their anxieties can they find ways to more productive living. (In passing—most urges for pleasure, if they are compulsive, including sex, are not caused by the wish for pleasure but by the wish for avoidance of anxiety.)

The problem of limits to consumption is so difficult to assess because, even in the affluent society of the United States, not all unquestionably legitimate needs are fulfilled. This holds true for at least 40 percent of the population. How can we even think of reduced consumption when the optimum consumption level has not been reached? The answer to this question must be guided by two considerations: first, that in the affluent sector we have already reached the point of harmful consumption; second, that the aim of ever-increasing consumption creates, even before the optimal consumption level is reached, an attitude of greed in which one wishes not only to have one's legitimate needs fulfilled but dreams of a never-ending increase in desires and satisfactions. In other words, the idea of the limitless rise of the production and consumption curve greatly contributes to the development of passivity and greed in the individual, even before peak consumption is reached.

In spite of these considerations, I believe that the transformation of our society into one which serves life must change the consumption and thereby change, indirectly, the production pattern of present industrial society. Such a change would obviously come not as a result of bureaucratic orders but of studies, information, discussion, and decision making on the part of the population, educated to become aware of the problem of the difference between life-furthering and life-hindering kinds of needs.

The first step in this direction would be studies which, to my knowledge, have never been seriously made, studies that would distinguish between these two kinds of needs. A group of psychologists, sociologists, economists, and representatives of the consuming public could undertake a study of those needs which are "humane," in the sense that they serve man's growth and joy, and those synthetic needs suggested by industry and its propaganda in order to find an outlet for profitable investment. As in so many other problems, the question is not so much the difficulty in determining the difference between these two types of needs and certain intermediate types but rather the raising of an extremely important question which can be brought up only if the social scientists begin to be concerned with man, instead of the alleged smooth functioning of our society or their function as its apologists.

One general consideration may be introduced at this point concerning the concept of happiness. The term "happiness" has a long history, and this is not the place to go into the meaning of this concept from its derivation from Greek hedonism to its contemporary usage. It may suffice to say that what most people experience as happiness today is really a state of full satisfaction of their desires regardless of their quality; if it is conceived in this sense, it loses the important qualifications which Greek philosophy gave it, namely, that happiness is not a state of fulfillment of purely subjective needs but of those needs which have an objective validity in terms of the total existence of man and his potentialities. We would do better to think of joy and intense aliveness instead of happiness. The sensitive person, not only in an irrational society but also in the best of all societies, cannot help being deeply saddened by the inevitable tragedies of life. Both joy and sadness are unavoidable experiences for the sensitive and alive person. Happiness in its present meaning usually implies a superficial, contented state of satiation, rather than that condition accompanying the fullness of human experience; "happiness" may be said to be the alienated form of joy.

How can such a change in the consumption and production pattern occur? To begin with, it is feasible that many individuals experiment with changes in this consumption pattern. To some extent this has already been done in small groups. The point here is not asceticism or poverty, but life-affirming as against life-denying consumption. This distinction can be made only on the basis of awareness of what life is, what activeness is, what is stimulating, and what their opposites are. A dress, an object of art, a house may be in the one or in the other categories. The dress which follows the fashion presented by the profit interests of the dressmakers and their public relations staffs is quite different from the dress which is beautiful or attractive and the result of personal choice and taste. A number of dressmakers might choose to sell their products to women who prefer to wear what they like rather than what is forced upon them. The same holds true of art objects, and all kinds of aesthetic enjoyment. If they lose their function as either status symbols or capital investments, the sense for the beautiful will have a chance for a new development. The unnecessary, or merely laziness-promoting, would be out. The private automobile, if it became a useful vehicle for transportation and not a status symbol, would change in significance. Certainly there would be no reason to buy a new car every two years, and industry would find itself forced to make some drastic changes in production. To put it in a nutshell: up to now the consumer has permitted and even invited industry to brainwash or control him. The consumer has a chance of becoming aware of his power over industry by turning around and forcing industry to produce what he wants or suffer considerable losses by producing what he rejects. The *revolution of the consumer* against the domination by industry has yet to come. It is perfectly feasible and its consequences far-reaching, unless industry takes control of the state and enforces its right to manipulate the consumer.

Speaking of the "revolution of the consumer" I do not have in mind that the consumer consider the corporation as his enemy whom he wants to destroy. What I have in mind is that the consumer challenge the corporation to respond to his wishes and that the managers begin to respond to this challenge. Accusations will not help to clarify or to improve the situation. Managers as well as consumers are part of the same alienated system; they are its prisoners rather than its creators. The managers tend to seduce the consumer into passiveness, but the consumer is attracted to his passive role; he makes it easy to be seduced. The resistance to basic change exists on both sides, but the wish for imaginative change, for liberation of energies, for new or creative solutions exists on both sides too.

A further measure would be legal restrictions on present methods of advertising. This point hardly needs an explanation. It refers to all semihypnotic and irrational advertising which has developed in the last decades. It could be effected by a simple law, like the one requiring cigarette manufacturers to put a warning of danger to health on their product,[13] or as fake and misleading advertising in interstate commerce and specifically false advertisements with respect to food, drugs, and cosmetics are forbidden by federal statutes.[14] Whether such a law has a chance to be passed against the combined powers of the advertising industry, the newspapers, television, radio, and, most of all, that part of industry for which hypnotic advertising is an im-

---

[13] While revising this manuscript, I read that a law is proposed by a federal agency which aims at the complete prohibition of cigarette advertising on television and radio.

[14] I appreciate a personal communication from Assistant Attorney General Frank W. Wozenkraft relating to existing laws.

portant aspect of its planning and production, depends on certain changes in our democratic process, and mainly simply on the question whether the citizen has a chance to be informed, to debate and to discuss this problem, and whether the power of citizens is superior to that of lobbies and those members of Congress who are influenced by lobbies.

What about a redirection of production itself? Assuming that the best experts and an enlightened public opinion came to the conclusion that the production of certain commodities is preferable to that of others in the interest of the population as a whole, could the freedom of the enterprise to produce that which is most profitable or requires least vision, experimentation, and daring be restricted within the framework of our Constitution? Legally this would not offer any great problem. While in the nineteenth century such change might have required the nationalization of industry, today it can be achieved by laws which require no change in our Constitution. The production of "useful" things could be furthered and the production of useless and unhealthy things could be discouraged by tax laws which favor those industries that agree to fit their production into the pattern of a sane society rather than into a pattern of "profit regardless." The government could influence adequate production by loans or, in certain instances, by government-owned enterprises which would pave the way for private initiative, once feasibility of profitable investment was proved.

Aside from all this, as a number of writers—particularly John Kenneth Galbraith—have emphasized, is the importance of increasing investment in the public sector in relation to investment in the private sector. All investments in the public sector—like public transportation, housing, schools, parks, theaters, and so on—have a twofold merit: first, of fulfilling needs adapted to man's aliveness and growth; second, of developing a sense of solidarity rather than one of personal greed and envy and hence competitiveness with others.

These remarks about consumption lead to one last point I wish to make in this connection—the connection between income and work. Our society, like many of the past, has accepted the principle "he who does not work should not eat." (Russian Communism has elevated this old principle into a "socialist" precept, phrasing it slightly differently.) The problem is not whether a man fulfills his social responsibility by contributing to the common good. In fact, in those cultures which have explicitly or implicitly accepted this norm, the rich, who did not have to work, were exempted from this principle, and the definition of a gentleman was a man who did not have to work in order to live in style. The problem is that any human being has an inalienable right to live regardless of whether or not he performs a social duty. Work and all other social obligations should be made sufficiently attractive to urge man to desire to accept his share of social responsibility, but he should not be forced to do so by the threat of starvation. If the latter principle is applied, society has no need to make work attractive and to fit its system to human needs. It is true that in many societies of the past the disproportion between the size of the population and the available techniques of production did not permit the freedom to dispense with the principle of what is, in fact, forced labor.

In the affluent industrial society there is no such problem, and yet even the members of the middle and upper classes are forced to follow norms laid down by the industrial system for fear of losing their jobs. Our industrial system does not give them as much leeway as it could. If they lose a job because they lack "the right spirit"—which means they are too independent, voice unpopular opinions, marry the "wrong" woman—they will have great difficulties in finding another job of equal rank, and getting a job of inferior rank implies that they and their families feel that their personality has been degraded; they lose the new "friends" whom they had gained in the process of rising; they fear the scorn of their wives and the loss of respect from their children.

The point I want to make is to uphold the principle that a person has an inalienable right to live—a right to which no conditions are attached and which implies the right to receive the basic commodities necessary for life, the right to education and to medical care; he has a right to be treated at least as well as the owner of a dog or a cat treats his pet, which does not have to "prove" anything in order to be fed. Provided this principle were accepted, if a man, woman, or adolescent could be sure that whatever he did his material existence would not be in jeopardy, the realm of human freedom would be immensely enhanced. Acceptance of this principle would also enable a person to change his occupation or profession by using one or more years in preparing himself for a new and, to him, more adequate activity. It happens that most people make a decision about their career at an age when they do not have the experience and judgment to know what activity is the most congenial to them. Perhaps in their mid-thirties they wake up to the fact that it is too late to start that activity which they now know would have been the right choice. In addition, no woman would be forced to remain unhappily married because she did not have what it takes even to prepare herself for a job at which she could make a living. No employee would be forced to accept conditions which to him are degrading or distasteful if he knew he would not starve during the time he looks for a job more to his liking. This problem is by no means solved by unemployment or welfare dole. As many have recognized, the bureaucratic methods employed here are humiliating to such a degree that many people are afraid of being forced into the dole-receiving sector of the population, and this fear is sufficient to deprive them of the freedom not to accept certain working conditions.

How could this principle be realized? A number of economists have suggested as a solution an "annual guaranteed income" (sometimes called a "negative income tax").[15] The guaranteed annual income would have to be definitely below the lowest income for work in order not to arouse resentment and anger in those who work. If it is to guarantee a modest but still adequate material basis, the present wage level would have to rise considerably. It is feasible to determine a minimum standard of living which is as high as the present minimum standard for a modest and adequate material basis. Anyone who is attracted by a more comfortable life would be free to achieve a higher level of consumption.

The guaranteed annual income could also serve, as some economists have observed, as an important regulating feature in our economy. "What we need," C. E. Ayres writes, "is some device that can be permanently instituted as a regular feature of the industrial economy by which demand can be made to keep pace with a constantly proliferating supply. The guarantee of a basic income to all members of the community irrespective of the earnings of employment, as Social Security payments are now guaranteed to all persons over seventy-two years of age, would provide the flow of effective demand that the economy more and more desperately requires." [16]

Meno Lovenstein, in a paper on guaranteed income and traditional economics, says: "An economist, even a traditional one, more likely than most people, should be able to view his analysis of the mechanisms of choices and see how limited, though essential, an instrument it is. As with so many proposals for new thinking, the concept of a guaranteed income should be wel-

---

[15] Cf. Robert Theobald, ed., *The Guaranteed Annual Income* (New York: Doubleday & Co., Inc., 1967); also proposals presented by Milton Friedman, James Tobin, and Representative Melvin Laird of Wisconsin, who is presenting a bill incorporating most of the features of Friedman's plan.

[16] C. E. Ayres, "Guaranteed Income: An Institutionalist View," in *The Guaranteed Annual Income*, Robert Theobald, ed. (New York: Doubleday & Co., Inc., 1967), p. 170.

comed as a challenge to theory before it needs to become a program for action." [17]

The principle of the guaranteed annual income has to cope with the objection that man is lazy and would not want to work if the principle of work-or-starve were to be abolished. In fact, this assumption is wrong. As overwhelming evidence shows, man has an inherent tendency to be active, and laziness is a pathological symptom. Under a system of "forced labor" where little attention is paid to the attractiveness of work, man seeks to escape from it if even for a short time. If the whole social system is changed in such a way that coercion and threat are removed from the work obligation, only a minority of sick people would prefer to do nothing. It is quite possible that a certain minority of people would prefer what would be the equivalent of the monastic life, devoting themselves completely to their inner development, to contemplation, or study. If the Middle Ages could afford to tolerate monastic life, certainly our affluent technological society is much more able to afford it. But again, as soon as we introduced bureaucratic methods necessitating that somebody had to prove that he really made "good use" of his time, the whole principle would be spoiled.

There is a specific variant of the principle of the guaranteed income which, although not likely to be accepted at present, constitutes an important principle. I am referring to the principle that the minimal requirements for a dignified life are not obtained on a cash basis, but as free commodities and services which do not require payment. We have accepted this principle for elementary schooling, nor does anyone have to pay for the air he breathes. One could begin to extend this principle to all higher education, which could be completely free, with a stipend for every student, making it possible for him to enjoy free access to education. We

---

[17] Meno Lovenstein, "Guaranteed Income and Traditional Economics," *ibid.*, p. 124.

could also extend the principle in another direction, namely, to have basic commodities free, beginning perhaps with free bread and free transportation. Eventually it could be extended to all commodities inasmuch as they constitute the minimum material basis for a dignified life. Needless to add, this vision is utopian as far as its realization in the near future is concerned. But it is rational, both economically and psychologically, for a much more advanced state of society.

To recommend that many affluent Americans begin to disconnect themselves from the endless and increasingly mindless process of more and more consumption requires at least a brief comment on the strictly economic implications of such a suggestion. The question is simply, Is it technically and economically possible for the economy to remain strong and stable in the absence of higher and higher consumption levels?

At this point American society is not affluent, at least for 40 percent of the population, and a large sector of the remaining 60 percent is not overconsuming. Hence, the question at this moment is not that of restriction of the growth of our production level, but of redirection of consumption. Nevertheless the question must be raised—whether, once the legitimate consumption level for the whole population has been reached, whatever it may be (including production which helps the poor nations), and considering the increase in production which corresponds to population increase, there is any point at which production would become stationary; or must we, for economic reasons, pursue the aim of a never-ending increase in production, which also means increase in consumption?

It is necessary that economists and planners begin to study the problem, even though at the moment it does not seem urgent from a practical standpoint. For as long as our planning is oriented toward the never-ending increase in production, our thinking and economic practices are influenced by this goal. This is already important in decisions about the rate of annual production growth. The aim of maximal economic growth rate is accepted like a dogma, undoubtedly because of the urgency of the real needs, and also because of the quasi-religious principle of the limitless rise in production as the goal of life called "progress," the industrial version of heaven.

It is interesting to note that earlier political economists writing in the nineteenth century saw clearly that the economic process of greater and greater production was a means to an end, not an end in itself. Once a decent standard of material life had been achieved, it was hoped and expected that productive energies would be redirected toward the truly human development of society. The goal of producing more material goods as the final and total end of life was foreign to them. John Stuart Mill wrote:

> Solitude, in the sense of being often alone, is essential to any depth of meditation or of character; and solitude, in the presence of natural beauty and grandeur, is the cradle of thoughts and aspirations which are not only good for the individual, but which society could ill do without. Nor is there much satisfaction in contemplating the world with nothing left to the spontaneous activity of nature; with every rood of land brought into cultivation, which is capable of growing food for human beings; every flowery waste or natural pasture ploughed up, all quadrupeds or birds which are not domesticated for man's use exterminated as his rivals for food, every hedgerow or superfluous tree rooted out, and scarcely a place left where a wild shrub or flower could grow without being eradicated as a weed in the name of improved agriculture. If the earth must lose that great portion of its pleasantness which it owes to things that the unlimited increase of wealth and population would extirpate from it, for the mere purpose of enabling it to support a larger, but not a better or a happier population, I sincerely hope, for the sake of posterity, that they will be

content to be stationary, long before necessity compels them to it.

It is scarcely necessary to remark that a stationary condition of capital and population implies no stationary state of human improvement. There would be as much scope as ever for all kinds of mental culture, and moral and social progress; as much room for improving the Art of Living, and much more likelihood of its being improved, when minds ceased to be engrossed by the art of getting on.[18]

In discussing consumption that does "little or nothing towards making life nobler or truly happier," Alfred Marshall states: "And though it is true that a shortening of the hours of labour would in many cases lessen the national dividend and lower wages; yet it would probably be well that most people should work rather less; provided that the consequent loss of material income could be met exclusively by the abandonment by all classes of the least worthy methods of consumption; and that they could learn to spend leisure well." [19]

It is easy to disqualify these authors as old-fashioned, romantic, etc. But the thinking and planning of alienated man may not be better just because it is the latest, or more in line with the programing principles of our technology. Precisely because we have today much better conditions for planning, we can give attention to ideas and values which we ridiculed from the standpoint of the mood of the first half of this century.

The theoretical question to be raised then is, Is a relatively stationary economic system possible under the conditions of modern technological methods, and if so, what are the conditions and the consequences?

I want to make only some general observations. If

[18] J. S. Mill, *Principles of Political Economy* (London: Longmans, Green & Co., 1929), pp. 750–751.

[19] Alfred Marshall, *Principles of Economics*, 8th edition (London: Macmillan, 1966), p. 599.

we were to cut back unnecessary dehumanizing consumption today, it would mean less production, less employment, and less income and less profit generated in certain sectors of the economy. Clearly, if this were done willy-nilly, with no planning, etc., it would cause extreme hardship for the economy as a whole and for specific groups of people. What would be required is a planned process of spreading the increased leisure across all areas of work, retraining of people, and a redeployment of some material resources. Time would be needed, and planning would of course have to be social rather than private, since no one industry could organize and implement a plan affecting wide sectors of the economy. Given proper planning, the reduction in total income and profit would not seem to be an insurmountable problem, since the need for income would have been reduced with the lowering of consumption.

As our productive potential has increased we have been faced with the choice of much less work with a constant level of production and consumption, or a much higher production and consumption with a steady level of work. Somewhat begrudgingly we have chosen a mixture of the two. Production and consumption have been increased, and at the same time work hours have been reduced and child labor largely abolished. This choice was not dictated by technical necessity, but was the result of changing social attitudes and political struggle.

Whatever the merits of these suggestions are, they are of little importance in comparison with what economists can suggest in response to the question, Is a stationary technological society possible?

The important point is that the specialists address themselves to this problem, and they will do so only if they see the relevance of the question. One should not forget that the main difficulty may be found not in the economic and technical aspects of the problem but in its political and psychological aspects. Habits and ways of thought do not bend easily, and since many powerful-interest groups have a very real stake in maintaining and speeding up the consumption treadmill, the struggle to change the pattern will be hard and long. As has been said many times, the all-important point at this time is that we make a beginning.

A final point on this: we are not alone in our fixation on material consumption—other Western nations, the Soviet Union, and East European nations also seem to be caught in the same destructive trap. Witness the Russian claim that they will bury us in washing machines, refrigerators, etc. The real challenge would be not to engage them in the wrong race, but to transcend this stage of social development and challenge them to build a truly human society—which will not be defined and measured by the number of cars or TV sets.

While this question of an eventually stationary production level is at the moment an essentially theoretical one, there is a very practical one which would arise if the consumers were to reduce their consumption to satisfy their real needs as living human beings. If this were to happen, the present rate of economic growth could be maintained if we redirected and transferred production from certain "unnecessary" private consumption to more humane forms of social consumption.

The needs here are clear and have been noted by many contemporary analysts and writers. A partial list of activities would include: a reconstruction of much of the nation's living space (millions of new housing units), a vast expansion and improvement in public education and public health, development of urban and intercity systems of public transportation, tens of thousands of small and large recreation projects in American communities (parks, playgrounds, swimming pools, etc.), a major beginning in the development of cultural life— bringing drama, music, dance, painting, movie making, etc., into hundreds of thousands of communities and millions of lives which currently have no real sense of this dimension of human existence.

All these efforts involve physical production and the

development of vast human resources. Such projects have the immediate virtue of attacking the problems of the impoverished minority, at the same time engaging the imagination and energies of the non-poor. They also soften, if not completely eliminate, the problems created by cutting back on consumption. National economic and social planning would, of course, be required if major programs of this kind were to be undertaken, since substantial shifts in the use of human and material resources would be involved. A prime result of such efforts would be to show that we were indeed moving toward a genuinely human community. Another great step in the direction of creating an alive, involved society would be taken if we guaranteed that in each aspect of such programs the people and communities involved would be responsible for project development and implementation. At the national level, enabling legislation is necessary plus adequate financing, but given this all-important minimum, maximum public participation and project diversity should be the prime principle.

In such a shift from the private to the public sector of consumption, private spending would be restrained as more income was diverted to higher taxes, and there would be a measurable shift from deadening, dehumanizing private consumption to new forms of public consumption that would involve people in creative community activities. Needless to say, such a shift would require careful planning to avoid severe upsets in the economic system; in this respect, we face the same problem in the conversion from armament to peace production.

5. PSYCHOSPIRITUAL RENEWAL

We have argued throughout this book that the system Man does not function properly if only his material needs are satisfied, thus guaranteeing his physiological survival, but not those needs and faculties which are specifically human—love, tenderness, reason, joy, etc.

Indeed, inasmuch as he is also an animal, man needs first to satisfy his material wants; but his history is a record of the search for and expression of his trans-survival needs, such as in painting and sculpture, in myth and drama, in music and dance. Religion was almost the only system which incorporated these aspects of human existence.

With the growth of the "new science," religion in its traditional forms became less and less effective, and there appeared the danger that the values which in Europe were anchored in the theistic frame of reference would be lost. Dostoevski expressed this fear in his famous statement: "If there is no God, everything is possible." In the eighteenth and nineteenth centuries, a number of people saw the necessity for creating an equivalent to what religion stood for in the past. Robespierre tried to create an artificial new religion and necessarily failed because his background of enlightened materialism and idolatrous worship of posterity did not permit him to see the basic elements which would have been needed for founding a new religion, even if it could have been done. Similarly, Comte thought of a new religion and his positivism made it equally impossible to arrive at a satisfactory answer. In many ways, Marx's socialism in the nineteenth century was the most important popular religious movement—though it was formulated in secular terms.

Dostoevski's prognosis of the breakdown of all ethical values if the belief in God ceased was only partly fulfilled. Those ethical values of modern society which are generally accepted by law and custom, such as respect for property, for individual life, and other principles, remained intact. But those human values which go beyond the requirements of our social order did, indeed, lose their influence and weight. But Dostoevski was wrong in another and more important sense. Developments during the last ten, and especially the past five, years all over Europe and in America have shown a very strong trend toward the deeper values of the humanistic tradition. This new quest for a meaningful life did not arise only among small and isolated groups, but became a whole movement in countries of entirely different social and political structures, as well as within the Catholic and Protestant churches. What is common to the believers and the nonbelievers in this new movement is the conviction that concepts are only secondary to deeds and human attitudes.

A Hassidic story might exemplify this point. The adherent of a Hassidic master is asked, "Why do you go to hear the master? Is it in order to hear his words of wisdom?" The answer is, "Oh, no, I go to see how he ties his shoelaces." The point hardly needs an explanation. What matters in a person is not the set of ideas or opinions which he accepts, because he has been exposed to them since childhood or because they are conventional patterns of thought, but the character, attitude, the visceral root of his ideas and convictions. The Great Dialogue is based on the idea that shared concern and experience are more important than shared concepts. This does not mean that the various groups referred to here have abandoned their own concepts or ideas or hold that they are not important. But they have all come to the conviction that their shared concern, their shared experience, their shared action causes them to have much more in common than what separates them by their unshared concepts. Abbé Pire has expressed it in a very simple and forceful way: "What matters today is not the difference between those who believe and those who do not believe, but the difference between those who care and those who don't."

This new attitude toward life can be expressed more specifically in the following principles: Man's development requires his capacity to transcend the narrow prison of his ego, his greed, his selfishness, his separation from his fellow man, and, hence, his basic loneliness. This transcendence is the condition for being open and related to the world, vulnerable, and yet with an experience of identity and integrity; of man's capacity to enjoy all that is alive, to pour out his faculties into the world around him, to be "interested"; in brief, to *be* rather than to *have* and to *use* are consequences of the step to overcome greed and egomania.[20]

From an entirely different standpoint, the principle shared by all radical humanists is that of negating and combating idolatry in every form and shape—idolatry, in the prophetic sense of worshiping the work of one's own hands and hence making man subservient to things, and in this process becoming a thing himself. The idols against which the Old Testament prophets fought were idols in stone or wood, or trees or hills; the idols of our day are leaders, institutions, especially the State, the nation, production, law and order, and every man-made thing. Whether or not one believes in God is a question secondary to whether or not one denies idols. The concept of alienation is the same as the Biblical concept of idolatry. It is man's submission to the things of his creation and to the circumstances of his doing. Whatever may divide believers and nonbelievers, there is something which unites them if they are true to their common tradition, and that is the common fight against idolatry and the deep conviction that no thing and no institution must ever take the place of God or, as a nonbeliever may prefer to say, of that empty place which is reserved for the No-thing.

A third aspect shared by the radical humanists is the conviction that there is a hierarchy of values in which those of the lower orders follow from the highest value, and that these values are binding and compelling principles for the practice of life—individual and social. There may be differences in the radicalism with regard to the

---

[20] It is well known that the principle outlined here is the basic one shared by Buddhist and Judeo-Christian thought. It is interesting that a Marxist philosopher, Adam Schaff, in his *Society and the Individual,* speaks of overcoming egotism as the basic principle of Marxist ethics.

affirmation of these values in the practice of one's life, just as there are in Christianity or in Buddhism among those who lead the monastic life and those who do not. But all these differences are relatively unimportant beside the principle that there are certain values which cannot be compromised. I submit that if people would truly accept the Ten Commandments or the Buddhist Eightfold Path as the effective principles to guide their lives, a dramatic change in our whole culture would take place. There is no need at this point to argue about details of the values which need to be practiced, for what matters is to gather those who accept the principle of *practice* rather than of *submission to an ideology*.

Another common principle is the solidarity of all men and the loyalty to life and to humanity which must always take precedence over the loyalty to any particular group. In fact, even this way of putting it is not correct. Any true love for another person has a particular quality: for I love in that person not only the person but humanity itself, or, as a Christian or Jewish believer would say: God. In the same way, if I love my country, this love is at the same time a love for man and mankind; and if it is not that, it is an attachment based on one's incapacity for independence and, in the last analysis, another manifestation of idolatry.

The crucial question is how these new-old principles can become effective. Those inside religion hope that they can transform their religion into the full practice of humanism, but many of them know that while this may prove to be true for some sectors of the population, there are others who for many obvious reasons cannot accept the theistic concepts and rituals so closely interwoven with them that it is almost impossible to separate the two. What hope is there for that part of the population which cannot even enter the ranks of the living Church?

Can a new religion be founded which has no premises such as those in Revelation, or any kind of mythology? Obviously religions are manifestations of the spirit within the concrete, historical process and the specific, social, and cultural circumstances of any given society. One cannot found a religion by putting together principles. Even the "nonreligion" of Buddhism cannot simply be made acceptable to the Western world, although it has no premises in conflict with rational and realistic thought and is basically free from all mythology.[21] Religions are usually founded by rare and charismatic personalities of extraordinary genius. Such a personality has not appeared yet on today's horizon, although there is no reason to assume that he has not been born. But in the meantime we cannot wait for a new Moses or a new Buddha; we have to make do with what we have, and perhaps at this moment of history this is all to the good because the new religious leader might too quickly be transformed into a new idol and his religion might be transformed into idolatry before it had a chance to penetrate the hearts and minds of men.

Are we then left with nothing but some general principles and values?

I do not believe so. If the constructive forces within industrial society which are choked by a deadening bureaucracy, by artificial consumption, and manipulated

---

[21] It has been emphasized by an important Czechoslovak philosopher, Fiser, in his significant and profound work on Buddhism (to be published) that Buddhism, aside from Marxism, is the only philosophy in history which has immediately seized the mind of the masses and as a philosophical system has developed into what in the West would be called a religion. But he also states that one cannot duplicate Buddhism and accept it in its existing form as a new religion for industrial society. This also holds true for Zen Buddhism, which is the most highly sophisticated, anti-ideological, rational, psychospiritual system I know and which developed all the forms of a "nonreligious" religion. It is not accidental that Zen Buddhism has aroused keen interest among intellectuals and especially among young people, and given rise to the hope that it could have a deep influence on the Western world. I believe its ideas can have that influence, yet it would have to undergo new and unpredictable forms of transformation to become the equivalent of a religion in the West.

boredom are released by a new mood of hope, by the social and cultural transformations discussed in this book, if the individual regains his confidence in himself, and if people make contact with each other in spontaneous and genuine group life, new forms of psychospiritual practices will emerge and grow which might be unified eventually in a total and socially acceptable system. Here, as well as with reference to many of the other points we have discussed, all depends on the courage of the individual to be fully alive and to seek solutions to the problem of his existence without waiting for the bureaucrats or the concepts to give him the answers.

It can even be hoped that certain forms of rituals become widely and meaningfully accepted. We see the beginnings of this, for instance, in songs like "We Shall Overcome," which are living rituals, not just songs. A ritual like that of common silence as it has been practiced by the Friends as the center of their religious service could become acceptable to large groups of people; it could become a custom that every meeting of significance begins or ends with five or fifteen minutes of common silence given to meditation and concentration. It is not too farfetched an idea to suggest that, instead of prayers or patriotic formulae, classes in schools and special occasions in universities could be introduced by a period of common silence.

We also have shared symbols, such as the dove and the outline of a human figure as symbols of peace and respect for man.

There is no point in speculating about further details of possible common rituals and symbols outside of church life, because they will grow naturally once the soil is prepared. I might add that in the field of art and music there are innumerable possibilities for the creation of new ritual and symbolic expressions.[22]

---

[22] It is interesting to note that Albert Schweitzer Colleges have organized a week of conferences in 1969 on the theme "Roads to a Revitalization of Religion Through the Arts."

Whatever new psychospiritual systems may arise, they will not be "fighting" religion, although they will be a challenge to those in the various religions who have made an ideology of religious teaching and an idol of God. Those who worship the "living God" will have no difficulty in sensing that they have more in common with the "unbelievers" than they have in what separates them; they will have a deep sense of solidarity with those who do not worship idols and who try to do what the believers call "God's will."

I expect that to many the hope expressed here for new manifestations of man's psychospiritual needs are too vague to form the basis of hope that such a development will happen. Those who want certainty and proof before they can take any hope seriously are right in reacting negatively. But those who believe in the reality of the yet unborn will have more trust that man will find new forms of expressing vital needs, even though at this moment there is only a dove with an olive branch indicating the end of the flood.

Chapter VI

Can We Do It?

1. SOME CONDITIONS

The changes suggested in the previous chapters are radical changes of the system projected twenty years into the future. The basic question is whether they can be accomplished within the present power structure, with democratic methods, and given present-day public opinion and mode of thought. Quite obviously, if they cannot be achieved, they are nothing but pious wishes or idealistic dreams. On the other hand, it ought to be clear that the question is not one of statistical probability. As I have indicated before, in matters of life—be it of the individual or of a society—it does not matter whether the chance for cure is 51 percent or 5 percent. Life is precarious and unpredictable, and the only way to live it is to make every effort to save it as long as there is a possibility of doing so.

The question, then, is not that it is certain that we can achieve these changes, or not even whether it is probable, but whether it is possible. Indeed, "it is part of the probability that the improbable happens," as Aristotle put it. The question is, to use a Hegelian term, of a "real possibility." "Possible" here means not an abstract possibility, a logical possibility, a possibility based on premises which do not exist. A real possibility means that there are psychological, economic, social, and cultural factors which can be demonstrated—if not their quantity, at least their existence—as the basis for the possibility of change. This chapter has the purpose of discussing the various factors which constitute such a real possibility for the accomplishment of the changes proposed in the previous chapter.

Before discussing these factors, I should like to stress certain means which are definitely not possible as a condition for change in the desired direction. The first one is that of a violent revolution in the style of the French or Russian revolutions, which means the overthrow of the government by force and the seizure of power by the revolutionary leaders. This solution is not possible for several reasons. First, there is no mass base for such a revolution. Even if all the radical students, including all the Negro militants, were in favor of it—which, of course, they are not—this mass base would be completely lacking because together they constitute only a very small minority of the American population. If a small, desperate group tried a *Putsch* or a kind of guerrilla warfare, its suppression would necessarily follow. Those who think in terms of a guerrilla war of the blacks against the whites in the cities forget Mao Tse-tung's basic insight that guerrillas can be successful only if they work within a population favorable to them. It need not be stressed that the real circumstances are precisely the opposite of this condition. Furthermore, it is most doubtful that even if the two factors mentioned so far did not exist, a violent revolution could succeed. A highly complex society like that of the United States, based on a large group of skilled managers and managerial bureaucracy, could not function unless equally skilled people took the place of those who run the industrial machine now. Neither the students nor the black masses offer many men with such skill. Hence, a "victorious revolution" would simply lead to the breakdown of the industrial machine of the United States and defeat itself, even without the forces of the state, which would suppress it. Veblen, in *The Engineers and the Price System,* already stated this essential point over forty-five years ago. He wrote: "No movement for the dispossession of the Vested Interests in America can hope for even a temporary success unless it is undertaken by an organization which is competent to take over the country's productive industry as a whole, and to administer it from the start on a more efficient plan than that now pursued by the Vested Interests; and there is no such organization in sight or in immediate prospect." [1] He adds an observation which is particularly relevant to today, when there is talk of a revolution by sabotage and guerrilla warfare. "Wherever the mechanical industry has taken decisive effect, as in America and in the two or three industrialized regions of Europe, the community lives from hand to mouth in such a way that its livelihood depends on the effectual working of its industrial system from day to day. In such a case a serious disturbance and derangement of the balanced process of production is always easily brought on, and it always brings immediate hardship on large sections of the community. Indeed, it is this state of things—the ease with which industry can be deranged and hardship can be brought to bear on the people at large—that constitutes the chief asset of such partisan organizations as the A.F. of L. It is a state of things which makes sabotage easy and effectual and gives it breadth and scope. But sabotage is not revolution. If it were, then the A.F. of L., the I.W.W., the Chicago Packers, and U.S. Senate would be counted among the revolutionists." [2]

And further: "To take effect and to hold its own even for the time being, any movement of overturn must from beforehand provide for a sufficiently productive conduct of the industrial system on which the community's material welfare depends, and for a competent distribution of goods and services throughout the community. Otherwise, under existing industrial conditions, nothing more can be accomplished than an ephemeral disturbance and a transient season of accentuated hardship. Even a transient failure to make good in the man-

---

[1] Thorstein Veblen, *The Engineers and the Price System* (New York: Harcourt, Brace & World, Inc., 1963), p. 97.
[2] *Ibid.*, p. 99.

agement of the industrial system must immediately defeat any movement of overturn in any of the advanced industrial countries. At this point the lessons of history fail, because the present industrial system and the manner of close-knit community life enforced by this industrial system have no example in history." [3]

It is important to consider the difference between the technical aspects of industrial society in 1968 and of Russian society in 1917, or even German society in 1918. These were societies which were by comparison much less complex and where, indeed, the apparatus of the government and of industry could have been taken over by intelligent and capable people from the outside. But 1968 in the United States is totally different from 1917 in Russia.

We touch again here on the problem of violence. It is a most amazing and bewildering paradox that in a situation where violence is losing its rationale—in international relations because of the existence of thermonuclear weapons and within a state because of the complexity of its structure—it is looked upon as a method of solution, although only by a small minority. This popularity of violence is an outcome of the psychic and spiritual despair and emptiness, and the resulting hate against life. It is greatly furthered by the literature which portrays man as driven to violence by his innate and almost uncontrollable destructive instinct.

On the other hand, the change in society cannot be accomplished simply by the publication of books advocating it or even by ideas spread by gifted speakers or orators. Unless such ideas can be translated into specific plans and actions, they may win the sympathies of a number of people who will, however, become all the more disappointed when they see that these ideas in themselves have had no influence on reality.

What, then, is the basis for the "real possibility"?

---

[3] *Ibid.,* p. 100.

Generally speaking, this real possibility can be formulated in a simple fashion: that it is possible to "move" public opinion to such a degree that it makes itself felt in the decision making of the executive and the legislative branches; that by its influence it restrains further expansion of the policies we are now embarked on; that eventually it gains a majority of voters; and thus that those who represent the ideas of the new movement become the political leaders of the country.

What are the conditions which form a real possibility to achieve this end? First of all, there are certain psychological conditions which have been on the increase for some time and which have become still more visible in the McCarthy campaign. I refer to the widespread dissatisfaction of people of all classes and ages with our way of life—its boredom and lack of joy. But this negative psychological condition would be much less effective if it were not for the presence of a positive condition, namely, that of a longing for new directions, for a renewal of values, for the end of the dehumanized, bureaucratic method, for a new psychospiritual orientation—longings which I have described in detail in the previous chapters.

The second condition is that our democratic system continues to function. Even though it does not live up to its promises, it is not insensitive to major swings in public opinion. Even our professional political bureaucracy—self-seeking as many of its members may be—wants to be re-elected and hence needs to pay attention to what people think and want. The first concrete condition, then, of achieving our aim is to preserve that minimum of democratic structure which we have got and to fight at every point where it is threatened.

The new constituency of the forces which want a new direction in American life exists already. It has such great power as a potential precisely because it is not restricted to one political party, social class, or age, but comprises a wide sector of the American population, from conservatives to radicals.

But this sector, while it may now comprise 25 percent of Americans—a conservative guess if one considers the effect of the McCarthy campaign and, to some extent, that of the Kennedy campaign [4]—would not be a strong enough influence for a drastic change of our policy. The question, then, is what are the chances for winning over the other 25 percent which would be needed. The objection seems obvious that, considering the power of the press, of the communications system, of the educational system, the large extent of brainwashing, it would sound quixotic to expect to increase the existing minority to the point where it becomes a majority. Perhaps the objection is somewhat less obvious if one thinks that ten years ago even the 25 percent would have seemed fantastic. At that time, one would have believed it to be utterly quixotic that a Senator without a nationally advertised name, without money, without the gimmicks which public-relations men often think are absolute requirements, could win or nearly win the Democratic primaries in states as diversified as California, New York, New Hampshire, and Oregon. But this argument, while not unimpressive, is certainly not enough to establish the real possibility for gaining a majority in the United States.

Among the conditions which make the victory of a new orientation a real possibility is the fact that the middle class has begun to listen and to be moved. Several elements have made this possible: material affluence has allowed the middle class to have the experience that more consumption is not the way to happiness. A higher educational level brings them into contact with new ideas and makes them more responsive to rational argument. Their comfortable economic situation makes them more aware of the many personal problems which they cannot solve. In the back of their minds is, often uncon-

---

[4] Together they won about 80 percent of the Democratic vote in the primaries in Oregon, California, and most others.

sciously, the question: Why is it that we, having everything one could wish, are unhappy, lonely, and anxious?
Is there something in our way of life, in the structure or
value system of our society, which is wrong? Are there
other and better alternatives?

In addition, there is another important factor: the
relationship of youngsters to their parents. It has happened again and again in recent years that young people
from twelve to twenty have confronted their parents
with their own doubts about the sincerity of what is
preached or about the sense of what is done, and a large
number of parents have been influenced by their children. While one might say that it is a regrettable sign
that parents don't believe in either an authoritarian or a
progressive value, this lack of belief has at least now the
great advantage that they can be converted by their
children, who, having gone through the experience of
disappointment and, not yet having acquired a resignation to falsehood and double-talk, confront their parents
with a deep contradiction within their own lives, very
often open their eyes and, not rarely, stimulate them and
activate them to a more sincere and less hopeless way of
looking at the world. Some have even gained a new interest in political action of which they had been despair-
ing before.

Perhaps the most important factor among those which
form the basis for the real possibility of change is one
which is not given enough weight in the general discussion. I mean the power of ideas. It may be necessary to
point out the difference between *ideas* and *ideologies*.
Ideologies are ideas formulated for public consumption,
satisfying the need of everybody to relieve his guilty
conscience in the belief that he acts in favor of something which appears good or desirable. Ideologies are
ready-made "thought-commodities" spread by the press,
the orators, the ideologists in order to manipulate the
mass of people for purposes which have nothing to do
with the ideology, and are very often exactly the op-

posite. Such ideologies are sometimes manufactured *ad hoc*—for instance, when a war is made popular by being described as a war for freedom, or when religious ideologies are used to rationalize the political *status quo* even though it may be in complete contrast to the genuine ideas of the religion in whose name the ideologies are preached. By its very nature, the ideology does not appeal to active thought, nor to active feeling. It is like a pill which either excites or puts man to sleep. Hitler saw this very clearly when he remarked in *Mein Kampf* that the best time for a public rally is the evening, when people are tired and most susceptible to influence. In contrast, the idea refers to what is real. It opens the eyes. It wakes men from their slumber. It requires them to think and to feel actively and to see something which they have not seen before. The idea has the power to awaken those who are exposed to it, provided it appeals to man's reason and all those other faculties which I have described in a previous chapter as "humane experiences." If the idea touches the people, it becomes one of the most powerful weapons because it creates enthusiasm, dedication, and increases and channels human energy. What matters is that the idea is not vague and general, but specific and enlightening and relevant to man's needs. The force of ideas becomes all the greater in a situation where those who defend the *status quo* do not have ideas, and this is precisely the case of the present situation. By the very nature of our bureaucracy and of the kind of organization which we encourage, at best we obtain bureaucratic effectiveness but no ideas. If we compare our situation with that in the middle of the nineteenth century, the fact cannot be ignored that the romantics and the reactionaries of the nineteenth century were full of ideas, very often profound and attractive ones—even though they may have been used for purposes which did not fulfill what the ideas promised. But today there are no ideas which help the defenders of the *status quo*. The latter repeat the old formulae of free enterprise, individual responsibility, law and order, honor of the country, etc., some of which are plainly in contrast to the reality to which they refer, and some of which are nothing but vague ideologies. It is a remarkable fact that today new ideas are to be found almost entirely among the people who are in favor of a basic change of the *status quo:* scientists, artists, and far-sighted men of business and politics. The great chance for those who want a new direction lies in the fact that they have ideas, while their opponents have outworn ideologies which may quiet people down but do not stimulate them or enhance their energies.

What about the mass media? Will they block the way to the spread of new ideas? It would be an oversimplification to say that, because the mass media support the establishment, they will block the publication of ideas which favor radical change. While the mass media are parts of the establishment, they also need customers and hence, just as the press needs to print news, they need to publish ideas which attract people, and they have to face the competition from new sources of news and discussion. Those who believe that the mass media are absolute obstacles to the spread of new ideas think in too doctrinaire and abstract a way and do not take account of the subtle realities which are inherent in the business of television, radio, and the press in a country like the United States. What might hold true for a country where the mass media are completely controlled by the state does not hold true to the same degree for the mass media who need to sell their products.

The spread of ideas fortunately is not entirely dependent on the favors of the mass media. The paperback has changed publication methods drastically. Many publishers are willing to publish ideas which find a sufficient number of readers—and that can be a small minority within the whole reading public—sometimes because they are interested in the idea itself, most of the time because they need to sell books. A paperback for sixty cents is as accessible economically as any number of the

mass-media magazines and can easily become a vehicle
to spread ideas provided the text is interesting and at-
tracts attention.

Another way of spreading ideas, which has already
been used to a considerable extent but which can still be
enhanced, is the method of news sheets, which are relatively cheap to publish and to send to a certain limited
public. Certain radio stations have also proved to have
given a much larger voice to new and progressive ideas
than others. On the whole, new technical factors work in
favor of the dissemination of new ideas. A variety of inexpensive printing techniques are developing, and inexpensive neighborhood radio stations can be organized.

Ideas become powerful only if they appear in the
flesh; an idea which does not lead to action by the individual and by groups remains at best a paragraph or a
footnote in a book—provided the idea is original and
relevant. It is like a seed stored in a dry place. If the
idea is to have influence, it must be put into the soil, and
the soil is people and groups of people.

Ideally speaking, the state and the Church are supposed to be the embodiment of social and religious ideas.
But this is true only in the most restricted sense. At best,
these organizations embody the minimum of the ideas
they proclaim. It is precisely for this reason that they do
not fulfill the function of helping the individual in the
development and realization of the values they proclaim.
Political parties today claim that they express values
and ideas more specifically than the state, but by their
bureaucratic structure and the need to make compromises, they fail to offer the citizen a place where he can
feel at home intellectually and spiritually; where he can
be active beyond the merely organizing-bureaucratic
functions. This view does not deny the importance of activity within political parties; it only claims that this
activity is not sufficient to give the individual a chance
to participate, to feel at home, and to become aware
that his ideas represent a style of life shared by others,
and expressed in common actions.

Furthermore, I do not believe that the forms of participatory democracy, which have been described in the previous chapter, are by themselves sufficient to bring about necessary changes. The face-to-face groups which I have described above must approach problems in a new spirit and with new ideas, but these ideas must be cultivated and spread so that they influence these groups.

2. A MOVEMENT

The conclusion seems unavoidable that the ideas of activation, responsibility, participation—that is, of the humanization of technological society—can find full expression only in a *movement* which is not bureaucratic, not connected with the political machines, and which is the result of active and imaginative efforts by those who share the same aims. Such a movement itself, in its organization and method, would be expressive of the aim to which it is devoted: to educate its members for the new kind of society in the process of striving for it.

In the following, I will try to describe three different forms of this movement.

The first step would be the formation of a National Council which could be called the "Voice of American Conscience." I think of a group of, say, fifty Americans whose integrity and capability are unquestioned. While they might have different religious and political convictions, they would share the humanist aims which are the basis for the humanization of technological society. They would deliberate and issue statements which, because of the weight of those who issued them, would be newsworthy, and because of the truth and rationality of their contents would win attention from at least a large sector of the American public. Such Councils could also be formed on a local level, dealing with the general questions but specifically with the practical questions relevant for the city or state which they represented. One could imagine that there might be a whole organization of Councils of the Voice of American Conscience, with a nationally representative group and many local groups following basically the same aims.

The National Council would deal with the broad aspects of national affairs, that is, foreign and domestic policies, while the local councils would take up the questions relevant to state and communities, again concerned with broad aspects rather than with details of execution. For example, the National Council would debate the question of the Vietnam war, our foreign policy in Asia, our assistance to the development of the poor nations, the reconstruction of our cities, the problems of values, education, and culture. The local councils would debate problems of conservation, city planning, slum clearance, relocating industries, etc. These debates would not be conducted on a general and abstract level. On the contrary, they would constitute the best thinking of the best minds in America. Often the Council would form subcommittees to study special problems and call upon specialists for advice. It would be up to the Voice of American Conscience (1) to clarify the issues, (2) to show the real possibilities and alternatives, (3) to recommend solutions, (4) to respond to statements and actions by other important social bodies, and to any criticism of their own recommendations. The examination of the issues and the recommended solutions would be rooted in the rationality and humanist values which the best in American culture stands for. These Councils would balance the structure based on political power represented by the government, the legislature, and the political parties. They would be the voice of reason and conscience, addressing themselves to the organs of power and to the population as a whole. Whenever the Councils did not arrive at unanimous solutions, one or more minority reports would be issued.

It is easy to underestimate what such Councils could do by pointing out that they would have no power. This is true in an obvious sense; it is not quite so true in a more subtle sense. Technological society, more than any society before, rests upon knowledge, on education in science and rational thought. While the average professional is not a true scientist but a mere technician, the development of scientific ideas depends on the development of the whole system of rational thought and reason. Development of technique has its basis in the development of scientific theory; this means that economic and political progress rest in the long run on the progress of culture. Those who represent culture have no direct power; but since the progress of society depends on their contribution, their voice will be taken seriously by a new class of people with college educations (teachers, technicians, programers, laboratorians, research workers, professionals, etc.) whose cooperation is a vital necessity for the functioning of the social system.

As to the composition of the Councils, they should not only represent various shades of political, religious, and philosophical convictions but also various fields of activities. Natural and social scientists, individuals from the fields of government, business, management sciences, philosophers, theologians, and artists should be among the members. But the foremost principle is the integrity and accomplishment of the members which override the principle of a well-balanced composition. It hardly needs to be added that the members of these Councils must be persons with a deep concern for the public weal, and hence willing to spend time and energy on their work in the Councils.

It is not too farfetched to think that the moral and intellectual weight of such groups could be of considerable influence on the thinking of Americans and by the freshness of its approach attract a great deal of attention.

How would the members of the Council be chosen? Quite obviously, they would not be elected as candidates are elected in a political party. And they couldn't very well be appointed by one supreme figure either, since that would give undue power to one individual. However, the formation of the National Council and of the local Councils appears to be so difficult only if one is caught in the old alternative between free election or arbitrary appointment. If one liberates oneself from these alternatives and thinks imaginatively, one will discover that there are methods which are perfectly feasible —although not as neat as the traditional ones. There are quite a number of people known for their integrity and achievement, and it would not be particularly difficult for a group of, let us say, ten to agree on the names of forty or fifty people who should be invited, by asking others who combine wisdom and intelligence what their preferences would be. Naturally, the forty or fifty people who were approached would themselves indicate who among those suggested were unacceptable to them, and what others they might suggest. As a result of this procedure, one might get a National Council which would not satisfy everybody and yet which would be fundamentally representative of the American conscience. The method of forming this Council is nonbureaucratic, personalistic, concrete, and, for this very reason, more effective than the traditional methods. The regional and local Councils could be formed in the same way, possibly aided by suggestions from the members of the National Council.

The Councils, of course, do not satisfy the needs which have been mentioned before: the need of the individual to work actively together with others, to talk, plan, and act together, to do something which is meaningful beyond the money-making activities of everyday life. To relate in a less alienated fashion than is customary in most relations to others, to make sacrifices, to put into practice norms and values in everyday life, to be open and "vulnerable," to be imaginative, to rely on one's own judgment and decision, the formation of a new type of social group is necessary.

I propose that this kind of shared activity and interest could occur on two levels: in larger groups of 100 to

300 [5] members who would form "Clubs," and in much smaller "Groups" of about 25 members, which would follow the same principle but in a much more intensive and absorbing way.

The Clubs should, if possible, be mixed in age and social class—but only experience would show to what extent practical considerations might make such a mixture difficult; it might be necessary that the Clubs be relatively homogeneous, but this defect could be made up for by an arrangement whereby Clubs with very different kinds of memberships could meet together regularly to exchange views and have personal contact. The Clubs should have a permanent meeting place; this could be a storefront or a basement—which is possible even in the poorest sections—or a school, church, or other building which could be rented at a fee contributed by the members. The meetings, which might take place once a week, should be meetings for exchanging information, discussion, and planning for the dissemination of the ideas of the movement. There should also be some relevant practical work undertaken by all members, such as participation in political campaigns, organization of discussion groups among neighbors and friends, engaging political leaders in public debates, problem-oriented care of public functions and community property, care of people—the old, children, and people in trouble—in the spirit of concern and stimulation rather than of bureaucratic methods. (It has been amply demonstrated that there are many people without degrees who, by their talent and skill, do as good or better work with and for others than the specialists. I mention as only one example Mayor John Lindsay's program for the rehabilitation of addicts in New York City; in this program specially gifted people—not pro-

---

[5] This number is arbitrary; what matters is that the size of the Club determines the exercise of its functions. One can also think of the possibility that one Club could have several sections.

fessional personnel—and former addicts have been very successful in the most important educative-therapeutic function.) The groups would have their own cultural life: showing movies, discussing books and ideas, dance, music, art—all of an active and nonconsumer type.

It is of the greatest importance that these Clubs try to have a style of their own, different from the style of traditional political or cultural clubs. The discussions should be led in such a way that the issues are clarified rather than obscured by phraseology and ideology. There must be a sufficient number of people in each Club who are aware of the pitfalls of language, are on the watch for obscuring or ideological language, and can teach how to think and to speak realistically. It is to be hoped that through this style of expressing oneself, the unnecessary misunderstandings and the accompanying defensive and attacking attitudes will be reduced considerably, and that people will learn to concentrate on their interest in what they are talking about rather than on their egos—which maintain opinions like flags that have to be defended. One would assume that out of this will develop personal contact more serious than that which is usual among conventional groups or even in what are often called personal friendships.

Needless to say, the organization of these Clubs must be free from all bureaucratic procedure. Each should have a chairman and a secretary, and these offices should change among the members every year. It would seem to be useful if once every six months or every year the representatives of the Clubs—say, one for each Club—could meet regionally and nationally in order to exchange experiences and to demonstrate to the rest of the population the value and fruitfulness of this type of organization.

They might be united by a loose and informal organization which helped to establish contact between the Clubs, responded to requests for advice and help, organized common meetings, and represented the Clubs to the public. But each Club should retain full autonomy, and be completely free from interference and control from above. Considering this autonomy, the various Clubs would differ a great deal among themselves and each individual could choose to join the Club whose spirit and program was most congenial to him. As to the formation of these Clubs, the only feasible way is that of spontaneous action. One or two persons who were seriously interested in the formation of a Club could invite five or ten others and from this nucleus a large group of from 100 to 300 persons might grow.

The question must be raised why the Clubs should not be a part of a political party, like Tammany Hall, for example, within the Democratic Party. There are mainly two reasons why this would be a mistake. The first and more obvious one is that none of the existing parties represents a philosophy and attitude like those that would underlie and be carried on by the Clubs. Both parties (and even a third party) would have members and sympathizers who shared the aims of the Clubs while they differed in their party affiliation. To have the Clubs politically unified would mean losing many people who either belong to another party or have no sympathy for political parties at all.

The second reason is based on the very nature of the movement and the Clubs. Their function would be not simply to influence political action, but to create a new attitude, to transform people, to demonstrate new ideas as they appeared in the flesh, as it were, of many groups of people, and thus to influence other people more effectively than is possible by political concepts. The new movement would be a cultural movement, aiming at the transformation of persons and of our whole culture; it would be concerned with socioeconomic and political matters, but also with interpersonal relations, art, language, style of life, and values. The Clubs are meant to be cultural, social, and personalistic centers, and hence to go far beyond what a political club could aspire to do; they would also arouse a greater or at least a different kind of allegiance than political clubs do.

While the Clubs would be basically different from political organizations, they would not be indifferent to politics. On the contrary, they would engage in clarifying and seriously discussing political issues; they would attempt to point to the real issues and to unmask deceptive rhetoric; their members would try to influence those political groups they might belong to and encourage a new spirit in politics.

There is also the possibility that a number of Clubs would spring from groups which already exist, like certain religious, political, or professional groups, and that the first Clubs would either consist mainly of the members of such groups, or that these members would form the nucleus of groups which would try to attract people outside of their own organizations.

I believe that these Clubs could form the basis for a mass movement of people. They would form a home for those who are genuinely interested in the aims of the movement and who want to further it, but who are not as totally and radically committed as a small number of people might be.

For this more radically committed minority, another form of common life and action seems desirable and necessary, which for the lack of a better word may be called "Groups."

Any attempt to spell out new forms of living or group activities such as the ones which are envisaged in the "Groups" must necessarily fail. To some extent this holds true even for describing the Clubs; but when we speak about the Groups who would try to achieve a new style of life, a new consciousness, a new language in a more radical way than the Clubs will do, the right words must be lacking to the same extent that the qualities of the life in the Groups are new. It is easier, of course, to say what the Groups would *not* be like. There has been a great deal of group activity emerging in recent years, from group therapy to "contact" groups to hippie groups of various kinds. The Groups envisaged here are very different. Their members would share a new philosophy, a philosophy of the love of life, its manifestations in human relations, politics, art, social organization. What would be characteristic of them is that none of these areas of human activities is isolated from each other, but each aspect gets its meaning by being related to all others.

These Groups would differ from the Clubs in the sense that each member would be willing to make greater sacrifices, and also to transform his personal life more profoundly in terms of the general principles of the movement. They should become a real home for every participant, a home where he finds nourishment in the sense of knowledge and of interpersonal sharing and, at the same time, where he has a chance to give. Their aim would be to move toward a personal transformation from an alienated person into one of active participation. Naturally, the Groups would be critical of the conduct of life as the alienated society offers it, but they would try to find an optimum of personal non-alienation rather than the solace of constant indignation as a substitute for being alive.

The Groups would develop a new style of life, unsentimental, realistic, honest, courageous, and active. It must be stressed that realistic unsentimentality—bordering, if you like, on cynicism—needs to be united with deep faith and hope. Usually the two are disconnected. People of faith and hope are often unrealistic, and the realists have little faith or hope. We shall find a way out of the present situation only if realism and faith become blended again as they were in some of the great teachers of mankind.

The members of the Group would speak a new language—English, of course, but an English which expresses rather than obscures, the language of a man who is the subject of his activities, not the alienated master of things which he manages in the category of "having" or "using." They would have a different style of consumption, not necessarily the minimum, but a meaningful consumption, one that serves the needs of life, not the needs of the producers. They would attempt to achieve personal change. Becoming vulnerable, active, they would practice contemplation, meditation, the art of being quiet, undriven, and ungreedy; in order to understand the world around them, they would try to understand the forces within themselves which motivate them. They would try to transcend their "ego" and to be "open" to the world. They would try to rely on their own thinking and feeling, to make their own judgments and take their chances; they would try to achieve an optimum of freedom, that is, of real independence, and give up the worship of and fixation on idols of any kind. They would overcome the incestuous ties to the past, to where they came from, to family and land, and replace them by a loving and critical concern. They would develop the fearlessness which only deep-rootedness in oneself, conviction, and a full relatedness to the world can give.

It goes without saying that the Groups would have their own projects that they would work on with intensity; their own cultural life; that they would educate themselves in the knowledge which our educational establishment fails to transmit; the relationship between the members would be the deep contact in which people allow themselves to be seen without armor or pretense— to "see," "sense," "read" each other without curiosity and intrusion.

I shall not speak about the various ways to reach these goals. Those who are serious about them will find out by themselves. For those who are not, anything further I could say would be just words which lead to illusions and misunderstandings.

Whether or not there are enough people who wish for a new form of living, and are strong and serious enough to form such Groups, I do not know. Of one thing, though, I am sure: if such Groups existed, they would exercise a considerable influence on their fellow citizens because they would demonstrate the strength and joy of people who have deep convictions without being fanatical, who are loving without being sentimental, who are imaginative without being unrealistic, who are fearless without depreciating life, who are disciplined without submission.

Historically, important movements have begun their lives in small groups. It does not matter whether we think of the early Christians, the early Friends, the Masons. I am referring to the fact that groups which represent an idea in its purity and without compromises are the seedbeds of history; they keep the idea alive, regardless of the rate of progress it makes among the majority. If the idea is no longer embodied "in the flesh," even if only of a small group, it is truly in danger of dying.

The Groups would be autonomous, yet connected to the Clubs by a loose common organization which would facilitate communication between the Groups and assist them in their work when the Group required it. Ideally, they would be composed of people of different age levels, education, social class, and, of course, color.

It is essential that the Groups not be based on particular formulations of concepts which one member has to accept in order to participate. What matters is the practice of life, the total attitude, the goal, and not a specific conceptualization. All this does not mean that the Groups should be inarticulate, that they should not discuss or even argue over concepts, but that what unites them is the attitude and action of every member and not a conceptual slogan to which he subscribes. The Group should, of course, have a general aim—which has been expressed before as the general aim of the movement. But they may very well differ considerably among themselves as to methods. I could imagine one Group which was in favor of civil disobedience and another which did not favor civil disobedience. Each individual would have a chance to join that particular Group whose attitude was most congenial to his own and yet be part of a larger movement which could even permit itself to have diversity as considerable as that between civil disobedience and its opposite.

As to the question of the relation between the Voice of the American Conscience, the Clubs, and the Groups, I would suggest that there be no formal bureaucratic relation, except perhaps that the Clubs and the Groups could draw on resources presented by a common office of information, and/or by a publication serving both Clubs and Groups. It seems also possible that individual members of the Groups would choose to work in the Clubs as their special project.

This whole outline of the movement is meant to be a very tentative proposal of how to begin. Maybe better ones will be made in debating these proposals. In fact, there are a large number of voluntary, purposeful, communal groups already existing, from whose experience a great deal can be learned. There is an ever-increasing tendency in the direction of individual initiative in group activity in all classes of the population, from student communities to farmers' organizations, like the National Farmers' Organization. There are purposeful agricultural communities, many of which are functioning successfully on the economic and the human plane, and there are many forms of community living in cities. Spontaneous formation of purpcseful groups has, in fact, deep roots in the American tradition. There is no lack of example and of data which would be helpful in building this movement.

The movement is conceived as an important element in the transformation of society which would allow the individual to find ways for immediate participation and action, and give an answer to his question: What can I do? It will allow the individual to emerge from his chronic isolation.

We are in the very midst of the crisis of modern man. We do not have too much time left. If we do not begin now, it will probably be too late. But there is hope—

because there is a real possibility that man can reassert himself, and that he can make the technological society human. "It is not up to us to complete the task, but we have no right to abstain from it." [6]

---

[6] Mischna, *Pirke Aboth*.

Epilogue

World Perspectives

It is the thesis of *World Perspectives* that man is in the process of developing a new consciousness which, in spite of his apparent spiritual and moral captivity, can eventually lift the human race above and beyond the fear, ignorance, and isolation which beset it today. It is to this nascent consciousness, to this concept of man born out of a universe perceived through a fresh vision of reality, that *World Perspectives* is dedicated.

Man has entered a new era of evolutionary history, one in which rapid change is a dominant consequence. He is contending with a fundamental change, since he has intervened in the evolutionary process. He must now better appreciate this fact and then develop the wisdom to direct the process toward his fulfillment rather than toward his destruction. As he learns to apply his understanding of the physical world for practical purposes, he is, in reality, extending his innate capacity and augmenting his ability and his need to communicate as well as his ability to think and to create. And as a result, he is substituting a goal-directed evolutionary process in his struggle against environmental hardship for the slow, but effective, biological evolution which produced modern man through mutation and natural selection. By intelligent intervention in the evolutionary process man has greatly accelerated and greatly expanded the range of his possibilities. But he has not changed the basic fact that it remains a trial and error process, with the danger of taking paths that lead to sterility of mind and heart, moral apathy and intellectual inertia; and even producing social dinosaurs unfit to live in an evolving world.

Only those spiritual and intellectual leaders of our epoch who have a paternity in this extension of man's horizons are invited to participate in this Series: those who are aware of the truth that beyond the divisiveness among men there exists a primordial unitive power since we are all bound together by a common humanity more fundamental than any unity of dogma; those who recognize that the centrifugal force which has scattered and atomized mankind must be replaced by an integrating structure and process capable of bestowing meaning and purpose on existence; those who realize that science itself, when not inhibited by the limitations of its own methodology, when chastened and humbled, commits man to an indeterminate range of yet undreamed consequences that may flow from it.

This Series endeavors to point to a reality of which scientific theory has revealed only one aspect. It is the commitment to this reality that lends universal intent to a scientist's most original and solitary thought. By acknowledging this frankly we shall restore science to the great family of human aspirations by which men hope to fulfill themselves in the world community as thinking and sentient beings. For our problem is to discover a principle of differentiation and yet relationship lucid enough to justify and to purify scientific, philosophic and all other knowledge, both discursive and intuitive, by accepting their interdependence. This is the crisis in consciousness made articulate through the crisis in science. This is the new awakening.

Each volume presents the thought and belief of its author and points to the way in which religion, philosophy, art, science, economics, politics and history may constitute that form of human activity which takes the fullest and most precise account of variousness, possibility, complexity and difficulty. Thus *World Perspectives* endeavors to define that ecumenical power of the mind and heart which enables man through his mysterious greatness to re-create his life.

This Series is committed to a re-examination of all those sides of human endeavor which the specialist was taught to believe he could safely leave aside. It attempts to show the structural kinship between subject and object; the indwelling of the one in the other. It interprets present and past events impinging on human life in our growing World Age and envisages what man may yet attain when summoned by an unbending inner necessity to the quest of what is most exalted in him. Its purpose is to offer new vistas in terms of world and human development while refusing to betray the intimate correlation between universality and individuality, dynamics and form, freedom and destiny. Each author deals with the increasing realization that spirit and nature are not separate and apart; that intuition and reason must regain their importance as the ·means of perceiving and fusing inner being with outer reality.

World Perspectives endeavors to show that the conception of wholeness, unity, organism is a higher and more concrete conception than that of matter and energy. Thus an enlarged meaning of life, of biology, not as it is revealed in the test tube of the laboratory but as it is experienced within the organism of life itself, is attempted in this Series. For the principle of life consists in the tension which connects spirit with the realm of matter, symbiotically joined. The element of life is dominant in the very texture of nature, thus rendering life, biology, a transempirical science. The laws of life have their origin beyond their mere physical manifestations and compel us to consider their spiritual source. In fact, the widening of the conceptual framework has not only served to restore order within the respective branches of knowledge, but has also disclosed analogies in man's position regarding the analysis and synthesis of experience in apparently separated domains of knowledge, suggesting the possibility of an ever more embracing objective description of the meaning of life.

Knowledge, it is shown in these books, no longer consists in a manipulation of man and nature as opposite forces, nor in the reduction of data to mere statistical order, but is a means of liberating mankind from the destructive power of fear, pointing the way toward the goal of the rehabilitation of the human will and the rebirth of faith and confidence in the human person. The works published also endeavor to reveal that the cry for patterns, systems and authorities is growing less insistent as the desire grows stronger in both East and West for the recovery of a dignity, integrity and self-realization which are the inalienable rights of man, who may now guide change by means of conscious purpose in the light of rational experience.

The volumes in this Series endeavor to demonstrate that only in a society in which awareness of the problems of science exists, can its discoveries start great waves of change in human culture, and in such a manner that these discoveries may deepen and not erode the sense of universal human community. The differences in the disciplines, their epistemological exclusiveness, the variety of historical experiences, the differences of traditions, of cultures, of languages, of the arts, should be protected and preserved. But the interrelationship and unity of the whole should at the same time be accepted.

The authors of *World Perspectives* are of course aware that the ultimate answers to the hopes and fears which pervade modern society rest on the moral fiber of man, and on the wisdom and responsibility of those who promote the course of its development. But moral decisions cannot dispense with an insight into the interplay of the objective elements which offer and limit the choices made. Therefore an understanding of what the issues are, though not a sufficient condition, is a necessary prerequisite for directing action toward constructive solutions.

Other vital questions explored relate to problems of international understanding as well as to problems dealing with prejudice and the resultant tensions and antago-

nisms. The growing perception and responsibility of our
World Age point to the new reality that the individual
person and the collective person supplement and integrate each other; that the thrall of totalitarianism of
both left and right has been shaken in the universal
desire to recapture the authority of truth and human
totality. Mankind can finally place its trust not in a
proletarian authoritarianism, not in a secularized humanism, both of which have betrayed the spiritual
property right of history, but in a sacramental brotherhood and in the unity of knowledge. This new consciousness has created a widening of human horizons beyond every parochialism, and a revolution in human
thought comparable to the basic assumption, among the
ancient Greeks, of the sovereignty of reason; corresponding to the great effulgence of the moral conscience artic-
ulated by the Hebrew prophets; analogous to the fundamental assertions of Christianity; or to the beginning of
the new scientific era, the era of the science of dynamics,
the experimental foundations of which were laid by
Galileo in the Renaissance.

An important effort of this Series is to re-examine the
contradictory meanings and applications which are given
today to such terms as democracy, freedom, justice,
love, peace, brotherhood and God. The purpose of such
inquiries is to clear the way for the foundation of a genuine *world* history not in terms of nation or race or
culture but in terms of man in relation to God, to himself, his fellow man and the universe, that reach beyond
immediate self-interest. For the meaning of the World
Age consists in respecting man's hopes and dreams
which lead to a deeper understanding of the basic values
of all peoples.

World Perspectives is planned to gain insight into the
meaning of man, who not only is determined by history
but who also determines history. History is to be understood as concerned not only with the life of man on this
planet but as including also such cosmic influences as

interpenetrate our human world. This generation is discovering that history does not conform to the social optimism of modern civilization and that the organization of human communities and the establishment of freedom and peace are not only intellectual achievements but spiritual and moral achievements as well, demanding a cherishing of the wholeness of human personality, the "unmediated wholeness of feeling and thought," and constituting a never-ending challenge to man, emerging from the abyss of meaninglessness and suffering, to be renewed and replenished in the totality of his life.

Justice itself, which has been "in a state of pilgrimage and crucifixion" and now is being slowly liberated from the grip of social and political demonologies in the East as well as in the West, begins to question its own premises. The modern revolutionary movements which have challenged the sacred institutions of society by protecting social injustice in the name of social justice are here examined and re-evaluated.

In the light of this, we have no choice but to admit that the *un*-freedom against which freedom is measured must be retained with it, namely, that the aspect of truth out of which the night view appears to emerge, the darkness of our time, is as little abandonable as is man's subjective advance. Thus the two sources of man's consciousness are inseparable, not as dead but as living and complementary, an aspect of that "principle of complementarity" through which Niels Bohr has sought to unite the quantum and the wave, both of which constitute the very fabric of life's radiant energy.

There is in mankind today a counterforce to the sterility and danger of a quantitative, anonymous mass culture; a new, if sometimes imperceptible, spiritual sense of convergence toward human and world unity on the basis of the sacredness of each human person and respect for the plurality of cultures. There is a growing awareness that equality may not be evaluated in mere numerical terms but is proportionate and analogical in its reality. For when equality is equated with interchangeability, individuality is negated and the human person extinguished.

We stand at the brink of an age of a world in which human life presses forward to actualize new forms. The false separation of man and nature, of time and space, of freedom and security, is acknowledged, and we are faced with a new vision of man in his organic unity and of history offering a richness and diversity of quality and majesty of scope hitherto unprecedented. In relating the accumulated wisdom of man's spirit to the new reality of the World Age, in articulating its thought and belief, *World Perspectives* seeks to encourage a renaissance of hope in society and of pride in man's decision as to what his destiny will be.

World Perspectives is committed to the recognition that all great changes are preceded by a vigorous intellectual re-evaluation and reorganization. Our authors are aware that the sin of *hubris* may be avoided by showing that the creative process itself is not a free activity if by free we mean arbitrary, or unrelated to cosmic law. For the creative process in the human mind, the developmental process in organic nature and the basic laws of the inorganic realm may be but varied expressions of a universal formative process. Thus *World Perspectives* hopes to show that although the present apocalyptic period is one of exceptional tensions, there is also at work an exceptional movement toward a compensating unity which refuses to violate the ultimate moral power at work in the universe, that very power upon which all human effort must at last depend. In this way we may come to understand that there exists an inherent independence of spiritual and mental growth which, though conditioned by circumstances, is never determined by circumstances. In this way the great plethora of human knowledge may be correlated with an insight into the nature of human nature by being attuned to the wide and deep range of human thought and human experience.

In spite of the infinite obligation of men and in spite

of their finite power, in spite of the intransigence of nationalisms, and in spite of the homelessness of moral passions rendered ineffectual by the scientific outlook, beneath the apparent turmoil and upheaval of the present, and out of the transformations of this dynamic period with the unfolding of a world-consciousness, the purpose of *World Perspectives* is to help quicken the "unshaken heart of well-rounded truth" and interpret the significant elements of the World Age now taking shape out of the core of that undimmed continuity of the creative process which restores man to mankind while deepening and enhancing his communion with the universe.

RUTH NANDA ANSHEN

To the Reader:

After having read this book you will understand that, and why, I am most interested to know your response to the special suggestions made in the last chapter. I would appreciate it if those who are interested would answer the following questions.

1. Three candidates whom I would propose for the National Council of the Voice of the American Conscience are:

    a) _____

    b) _____

    c) _____

2. I am interested in participating in a Club:

    a) I wish to participate _____yes _____no

    b) I would consider it _____yes _____no

    c) I want to be kept informed _____yes _____no

    d) Suggestions _____

    _____(use extra page if needed)

3. I am interested in participating in one of the Groups:

    a) I wish to participate _____yes _____no

    b) I would consider it _____yes _____no

    c) I want to be kept informed _____yes _____no

    d) Suggestions _____

    _____

4. General comments or suggestions _____

    _____

    _____(use extra page if needed)

Please cut out this page and mail it to me, c/o Bantam Books, Inc., 271 Madison Avenue, New York, N.Y. 10016. I have not provided a pre-paid envelope; the reason follows from what is said in the book. Even the first small step requires the initiative at least to address the envelope yourself and spend the money for a stamp.

Erich Fromm